Everyone Reads!

Simple and Effective Strategies for Children with a Variety of Reading Difficulties

by
Sherrill B. Flora

illustrated by
Julie Anderson

Publisher
Key Education Publishing Company, LLC
Minneapolis, Minnesota

CONGRATULATIONS ON YOUR PURCHASE OF A KEY EDUCATION PRODUCT!

The editors at Key Education are former teachers who bring experience, enthusiasm, and quality to each and every product. Thousands of teachers have looked to the staff at Key Education for new and innovative resources to make their work more enjoyable and rewarding. Key Education is committed to developing and publishing educational materials that will assist teachers in building a strong and developmentally appropriate curriculum for young children.

PLAN FOR GREAT TEACHING EXPERIENCES WHEN YOU USE EDUCATIONAL MATERIALS FROM KEY EDUCATION PUBLISHING COMPANY, LLC

CREDITS
Author: Sherrill B. Flora
Cover Design: Annette-Hollister-Papp
Illustrations: Julie Anderson
Editors: George C. Flora, Audrey Rose
Photography © by: Banana Stock,
Brand X, Comstock,
Digital Vision, and
Photodisc

Key Education welcomes manuscripts and product ideas from teachers.
For a copy of our submission guidelines, please send a self-addressed, stamped envelope to:

Key Education Publishing Company, LLC
Acquisitions Department
9601 Newton Avenue South
Minneapolis, Minnesota 55431

Contents

Research-Based Conclusions: The Prevalence of Reading Difficulties and Disabilities

In today's schools, an increased importance is being placed on strong literacy skills and on academic performance. Children are routinely evaluated through standardized testing and compared against the "norm" or "average." Teachers are being challenged to find the best teaching methods that will reach the majority of their students.

Children who have reading difficulties, such as dyslexia, or other related reading disorders or learning disabilities, are far more prevalent than what was once believed. According to the 1998 large scale test results of the National Assessment of Educational Progress (NAEP) and the U.S. Department of Education, it was determined that 69 percent of fourth graders and 67 percent of eighth graders were reading below grade proficiency levels.

Moreover, according to the NAEP data, as many as 38 percent of fourth graders had not achieved even rudimentary skills in reading. This horrific data led the Committee on Prevention of Reading Difficulties in Young Children of the National Research Council to conclude: "The educational careers of 25 to 40 percent of American children are imperiled because they don't read well enough, quickly enough, or easily enough." This data also provided statistical support that shows that one in five students are likely to have problems learning to read.

Further research has provided evidence that there is a significant difference in how children are being identified as "reading disabled" by our schools.

It has also been found that less than a third of the children who were reading below age or grade level were receiving special services for their reading difficulties. This strongly suggests that our schools have many children with undiagnosed disabilities and potential reading problems.

Even when school identification of reading problems takes place, it often occurs late in a child's educational experience. Children with dyslexia are generally not identified until third grade or beyond. The later the identification, the more difficult the problems are to remediate. These children have already fallen significantly behind their peers in achievement, thereby causing them to experience patterns of failure, such as a loss of self-esteem, a dislike of reading and school, and feelings of being overwhelmed by the number of skills that must be learned in order to "catch-up" with their classmates.

This research has highlighted the need for greater responsibilities for preschool, kindergarten, first grade, and second grade teachers. These teachers are already engaged in early reading intervention, whether they realize it or not. One in five of their students—20 percent—will have difficulty learning how to read. The good news is that with early intervention, appropriate instruction, and remedial follow-up, many of these children can become successful readers and may never experience the overwhelming feelings of failure.

A Checklist: Children Who May Have Trouble Learning to Read —

—————— Kindergarten and Grade One Warning Signs ——————

The majority of children with reading disabilities are generally not identified until third grade or later. To improve on this, the observations of kindergarten and first grade teachers are now even more crucial. There are many early signs that can be observed during these first years of school. These warning signs could alert you to those children who may have significant trouble learning how to read:

- **Poorly developed fine motor skills.** These skills are noticeably less mature than the majority of other children who are the same age. For example, they include far fewer details in their drawings.

- **Sitting and listening to stories is not a rewarding experience.** These children would rather ramble or move from activity to activity.

- **Difficult time sequencing story events.** When listening to a story, these children will either miss or rearrange key events.

- **A lack of interest in rhyming words and nursery rhymes.** This can signal an inability to hear phonemes. Some children do not seem to comprehend that words can be separated into individual sounds.

- **Immature speech and/or articulation difficulties.** Immature speech is not uncommon among incoming kindergartners. However, there are specific signals that teachers can listen and look for, such as spoken words where letters (either beginning or ending sounds) are being dropped or when speech resembles "baby talk."

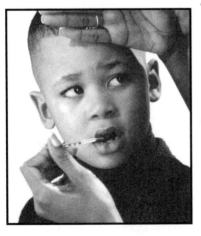

- **Poor communication skills.** These children may not be able to recall common vocabulary when asking for things or when expressing a need. They seem to lack general knowledge and often take a long time when trying to give or recall information.

- **Difficulty in learning and remembering letter names.** Some children may even struggle to learn the letters in their own names.

- **Complains that reading is hard.** Some children may express frustration or may even begin to feel ill at reading time.

What To Look For:
Observable Characteristics
that Accompany Dyslexia and Other
Developmental Reading Disorders

The Problems

The following is a list of observable behaviors that children with dyslexia or other developmental reading disorders may exhibit. All children—even those who have been identified as having dyslexia—will not have the exact same problems or strengths. Children with reading difficulties have their own unique learning styles. The following list comprises just some of the problems that can be observed in children who are at risk of reading failure:

- **Delayed speech.** This can be subtle and go unnoticed or it may be quite pronounced.

- **Articulation errors.** Speech patterns may strongly resemble baby talk.

- **Mishears phonemes.** While speaking, the child will leave off beginning or ending sounds.

- **May substitute phonemes.** For example, the child may say "car" for "cap,"—a word that makes no sense in context.

- **Does not hear or enjoy rhymes or rhyming words.**

- **Forgets or cannot recall words.** The child may ask for "something" rather than using the actual name of the desired object.

- **Difficulty in expressing ideas, thoughts, and observations when talking.**

- **Confusion with left- and right-handedness.**

- **Difficulty in learning the names and sounds of alphabet letters.** This underdeveloped skill prevents children from "sounding out" unknown words.

- **Lack of awareness of the sounds in spoken words, sound order, and the sequence of syllables.**

- **Difficulty in decoding words (letter-sound correspondences) and with single sight word recognition.**

- **Difficulty with encoding words.** These children struggle with the correspondence of sounds to letters when spelling words.

- **Poor sequencing of numbers and letters in words when read or written.** For example, the child may reverse b as d, p as q, was for saw, or invert W as M, 12 as 21, or sign as sing.

- **Problems with reading comprehension.**

- **Confusion with directions in time and space.** For example, these concepts include right and left, up and down, and yesterday and tomorrow.

- **Dyslexia runs in families.** Similar problems may be noticed in other family members.

- **Difficulty with handwriting.**

The Strengths

It is also important to look for each child's strengths. Understanding a child's strengths better enables the teacher to plan direct-instruction lessons that have a higher probability of attaining success.

It is extremely important to note that most children with a developmental reading disorder or dyslexia have normal intelligence, and many have above-average intelligence. A reading disability is a specific information processing problem that is not connected to the ability to think or to comprehend complex higher-order thinking.

These children simply have brains that are "wired" a little differently which creates unique learning styles. While these disabilities may present certain difficulties, they are also associated with many talents and strengths. For example:

- These children are often creative thinkers, highly imaginative, and may excel in drama, art, or music.

- Many of these children have superior reasoning abilities that can be observed when they play games of strategy, build with construction materials, and solve complicated puzzles.

Instead of viewing dyslexia or developmental reading disorders simply as disabilities, view them also as individual learning styles. All children have different learning styles, unique strengths, and varying ways that they perceive, organize, conceptualize, and recall information.

Using a multi-sensory approach that combines visual, auditory, and tactile experiences will simultaneously provide all of the children in a class with the opportunity to utilize their most dominant learning style. This instructional method offers children the most comprehensive reading experience.

Multi-sensory activities that involve seeing, speaking, listening, and touching are designed to help children learn to read faster—not only children who are struggling—but all of the children in your classroom.

Teach to strengths —
provide many and varied experiences —
and you will see greater success
and happier children!

Visual and Auditory Processing Difficulties of Children with Learning Disabilities

Children with learning disabilities usually have difficulty in how they process information. Each type of processing difficulty creates a different type of learning (and teaching) challenge. By knowing how to identify these processing difficulties, and by understanding how those challenges can affect how children learn, teachers are better equipped to plan instructional activities that help these children process information to the best of their abilities.

The following lists provide an overview of specific processing difficulties and how they affect children. The following chapters provide suggestions for modifying techniques and instructional lessons that will assist in teaching to the strengths, and not the weaknesses, of these children.

Visual-Motor Difficulties
- General poor motor coordination
- Poor perception of time and space, (before and after, up and down, yesterday and tomorrow)
- Gets lost easily
- Exhibits directionality problems
- Poor fine motor skills—difficult time coloring, drawing, cutting, and pasting
- Poor handwriting—letters are often jumbled, with little spacing between letters
- Short attention span
- Clumsy, trips frequently, may have trouble learning how to alternate feet on stairs or learning how to skip
- Difficult time learning directional concepts (over, under, behind)

Visual-Memory Difficulties
- Difficulty with spelling
- Inconsistent word identification
- Difficult time learning to print alphabet letters and numbers
- May have letter reversals or inversions

Visual-Discrimination Difficulties
- Unable to retell a story from pictures
- Letter and number association is slow to develop
- Difficult time comprehending written directions
- Needs auditory directions and cues
- Skips lines when reading
- Rereads sentences or parts of sentences
- Easily loses spot on the page
- May complain that eyes hurt

KE-804026 © Key Education   11   *Everyone Reads!*

Auditory-Memory Difficulties
- Difficulty remembering oral directions
- Difficult time memorizing nursery rhymes
- Difficult time learning the alphabet and numbers
- Difficult time with all rote memory skills

Auditory-Discrimination Difficulties
- Does not appear to be listening or paying attention
- Difficult time memorizing nursery rhymes
- Difficult time learning the alphabet and numbers
- Often does not enjoy being read to
- Slow to respond
- Often avoids participating in class
- Often does not distinguish between sounds in letters or in words
- Difficult time understanding verbal questions
- May mispronounce words
- Needs picture cues
- Information must be repeated and spoken slowly

Benefits and Components of a Balanced Reading Program

The National Reading Panel (NRP) convened by the National Institute of Child Health and Human Development (NICHD) and the Department of Education found that instructional programs that provided systematic instruction in phonemic awareness, phonics, guided reading to improve fluency, and direct instruction in vocabulary and reading comprehension skills were significantly more effective than approaches that were less focused on reading skills. This is also the system that works best for the majority of the children who are struggling in school.

The following is a comprehensive list of elements that should be incorporated into a strong and balanced literacy program:

- Reading aloud to children daily

- Varied shared book and writing experiences

- Phonemic awareness experiences

- Systematic phonics instruction and practice

- Oral language development

- Activities to strengthen listening skills

- Organized vocabulary development

- Guided reading

* Silent reading

- Individualized reading lessons

- Model writing skills

- Daily writing experiences

- Practice in rewriting and editing

- On-going evaluation of student progress

- Opportunities to use print in meaningful daily living experiences.

Getting Started and Getting Organized: Strategies to Improve Work Habits and Organizational Skills

Most struggling learners and children with reading disabilities have unique and varied learning styles which will affect how they learn to read. These same children often have poor organizational skills and work habits that can also severely interfere with learning.

To be most effective, teachers must use a wider range of methods and materials for teaching reading, and they must also examine how they have organized the materials and furniture in their classrooms, how their daily routines are scheduled, and how they have decided to teach good work habits. Considering all these elements will create the optimum learning environment for these children.

Teachers also need to find ways to help these children develop better school survival skills. Work habits and organizational skills are life skills! The strengthening of these skills will help children in everything they attempt to do—generating great feelings of success! And children who feel successful are simply happier and do better in school!

Schedules and Communication

- **Routines are incredibly important**—especially for children who have trouble remembering the sequence of the day. Ensure that a daily schedule is maintained. Provide children with their own copies of the schedule. For nonreaders, use picture clues; numbers for math time; a picture of a book for reading; and a lunch box for lunchtime. These visual clues will help children feel more secure when they know what will be happening.

- **Verbal clues.** Provide verbal clues to the students to ensure that they are prepared and know what is coming next. Provide constant and immediate feedback. Catch them right away when they are doing well as well as when correction is needed.

- **Communicate regularly with parents.** Make sure you keep a positive home-school connection. Sending journals back and forth can be extremely worthwhile. This also encourages parents to communicate with the school staff.

- **A daily assignment book**. A daily assignment book, even for nonreaders, is an excellent tool to help the child become more organized, as well as keeping parents informed. Parents can be asked to initial the book daily. This lets the teacher know that they discussed school work with their child and ensures that the child has brought information home to parents. The routine of a daily assignment book can teach children to be responsible for carrying home information and help them remember to complete tasks.

Work Habits and Task Completion

- **Shorten assignments.** Provide frequent but shorter assignments to guarantee completion, and to establish the "habit" of completing tasks.

- **Reward charts.** Allow the children to keep "work completed charts" taped to their desks or assigned work areas. Every time a task is completed the child can earn a sticker that can be exchanged later for another reward, such as lunch with the teacher or a new pencil.

- **Assign tasks that you know the child will be able to successfully complete.** Building on success will help the child gain confidence as tasks become more difficult.

- **Encourage good school attendance.** Children who attend school regularly have a better chance of achieving their maximum potential. Children with poor attendance find it even more difficult to keep up with their peers.

- **Stress punctuality.** Learning how to be on time and prepared to learn can be fun. Create a make-believe time clock in your classroom or have the student sign a time card. School is their job and it is their responsibility to arrive on time and be ready to learn.

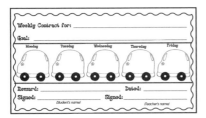

- **Use "contracts."** Take the time to explain, write down, and have both the teacher and the student sign a contract stating the behavior and learning expectations. This can be a very effective educational tool—even with very young children. See page 21 for two reproducible contracts.

Working with Others

- **Peer tutors.** Peer tutors can be extremely effective when the children are respectful of one another. Establishing relationships with other children in the classroom is very important for the child who is struggling.

- **Assign small group projects.** Make sure that the struggling student is assigned a part of the project that will allow the child to excel. For example, if the struggling reader is a good artist, suggest that the graphs or illustrations be completed by that child.

- **Assign "partner" or "team" jobs in the classroom.** Partners can take attendance to the office; care for a classroom pet; erase blackboards; or care for classroom plants. Using words like "partner" or "team" helps the children to feel connected and realize that the job and the "partnership" is important.

Specific Accommodations and Modifications for Working with Struggling Students in the Classroom

Every classroom—in every state and province—have student populations of great diversity: diversity in learning styles, in academic abilities, in students' interest levels, and in students' home-lives and cultural backgrounds. Every classroom will have children who need special attention and who will benefit from teachers who take the time to make certain accommodations and modifications in the classroom.

Not all techniques and methods work with all children. Often it is a process of trial and error to discover what are the most successful techniques for individual students. The following classroom-tested suggestions have been found to be valuable for assisting teachers in managing a variety of special education needs and for helping young learners to experience greater success in the regular education classroom.

Adjustments and Modifications for Schedules, Student Groups, Room Arrangement, and Classroom Work Space

- **Stay close.** Early in the year, have these children sit closer to you for more positive feedback and to ensure that they have a clear understanding of assignments and expectations.

- **Quiet work areas.** Establish a quiet corner somewhere in the classroom, such as a study carrel, that is free from all distractions (visual and auditory). This space should never be associated with negatives consequences. This should be a special place where children will want to sit and work.

- **Keep desk clear and clean.** Help children learn to keep their desks free of unnecessary materials. Cluttered desks create undue confusion and disorganization for a child who already has difficulty organizing materials.

- **Take frequent short breaks.** Struggling learners can find taking frequent short breaks to be beneficial. A few seconds to get a drink of water or simply to stand up and walk around the room can be refreshing for children who find it difficult to sit for long periods of time.

- **Alternate various activities.** Alternate the types of activities and lessons presented in the classroom. For example, plan an activity that involves movement and active participation and then follow that lesson with a quiet activity. This type of variety helps children to maintain interest.

- **Separate distracting students.** Separate struggling students from other students who may be distracting to them. Sit children by others who can be helpful and where positive relationships can be established.

- **Match children with complementary strengths.** Pair the children into "work-teams." Match children with complementary strengths. For example, an auditory learner could work with a visual learner. The children will be able to share what they are best at while helping each other.

- **Work Contracts.** Work contracts can also be effective tools for helping children to improve task completion and for better understanding expectations. (See work contract samples on page 21.)

Adjustments and Modifications for Lesson Presentation and Types of Instructional Materials

The following ideas can be beneficial techniques for helping most struggling learners:

- **Provide frequent reminders and praise efforts and accomplishments often.**

- **Measurable and attainable assignments.** Make sure that the assignments are specific, measurable, and can be completed by the child.

- **Stand close to the distracted learner when giving oral directions.** A child who sits in the back of the room or who is easily distracted may not even notice that the teacher has given a new direction.

- **Shorter assignments and work periods.** By providing shorter assignments and shorter work periods can give the children a sense of completion and success. As children become more confident as learners, the length of both assignments and work periods can be extended.

- **Look at and correct papers frequently.** Students need immediate feedback.

- **Allow the children time to ask questions and seek clarification.** Remember, these children are often slow to formulate responses.

- **Cut or fold papers in half.** Students can easily be overwhelmed by assignments that appear to be long or overly crowded. Many children even appreciate receiving papers that are folded into fourths. It is rewarding for the students to feel as if they have completed something before moving on to the next task.

- **Provide alternatives to replace paper and pencil tasks.** Use audio tapes, oral reports, or illustrations as examples. (See page 20 for alternative learning materials.)

- **Copy chapters of textbooks and/or provide students with two copies of assignments.** Having copies allows the child the opportunity to underline, highlight, and make notes right on the assignment.

- **Use graph paper.** The use of graph paper works well for organizing mathematical problems and for writing out spelling words.

- **Provide as many visual, auditory, and tactile representations as possible.**

- **Computers and word processors.** Encourage the children to become comfortable and proficient at using a word processor. Children with handwriting difficulties, as well as visual learners, find word processors to be very effective teaching aids.

Specific Adjustments and Modifications for Auditory Learners

The following ideas can be beneficial for children who are primarily auditory learners:

- **Provide clear oral directions.** Auditory learners need to hear directions as well as be provided with the written directions for assignments.

- **Tape record text.** Individual tape recorders can be effective tools in the classroom. Children can record directions and replay them later. Stories, textbook chapters, and other written information can also be recorded and played back as needed.

- **Have students make their own recordings.** The students can record their own information into a tape recorder. This provides children with recorded information that can be played again, and it gives the children the opportunity to hear themselves speak the information, which helps children to internalize what they are learning.

- **Let children take turns drilling each other.** This creates a nice social interaction and allows the auditory learner to speak and hear the information.

- **Teach the children how to close their eyes and quietly "hear in their heads" the information that they want to recall.**

- **Use films, books on tape, and computer games with sound.** These are all beneficial teaching tools for the auditory learner.

Specific Adjustments and Modifications for Visual Learners

The following ideas can be beneficial for children who learn best visually:

- **Visual learners need to learn how to turn words and information into visual images.** (See pages 43 to 52.)

- **Flash cards printed in bright colors.** These are fun to look at and will make the work more interesting.

- **Provide visual clues.** Use visual clues for all directions and information. Make frequent use of the chalkboard or wipe-off board.

- **Self-stick adhesive notes.** These can be a valuable tool for visual learners. Encourage note taking and then stick the note near the needed information. Self-stick notes also make for great visual reminders of tasks that need to be completed, such as daily homework assignments.

- **Graphic organizers.** Graphic organizers can be useful for helping children organize and remember information. (See pages 65 to 81.)

- **Vary paper-and-pencil tasks.** Visual learners respond well to completing tasks that utilize a variety of art materials: crayons, cut-and-paste materials, magazine and newspaper collages, and colored pencils are just a few examples.

Specific Adjustments and Modifications for Testing and Evaluations

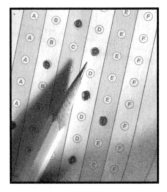

- **Hold frequent conferences with children.** Let them know how they are succeeding and what areas still need work. Allow the child time to ask questions and talk about areas of frustration.

- **Underline the key direction words on tests.** Often times, children do not complete the work correctly because they have misread or misunderstood the directions.

- **Do not time the tests.** Children work better without the pressure of knowing that their work time could run out.

- **Allow these students to take tests in small sections over an extended period of time.**

- **Allow for flexible sitting.** Many children work better alone and without distractions.

Alternative Learning Materials
(more than pencil and paper tasks)

audio tapes
bulletin boards (interactive)
brainstorming
chalkboards
clay or play dough
comic books
computers
CD player
demonstrations
displays
dramatic presentations
field trips
films
filmstrips
flannel boards
flip charts
glitter glue
graphic organizers
hands-on games
homework assignments
magnetic boards
magnetic letters

models
oral presentations
overhead projector
peer tutors
photographs
poetry
posters
puppets
read aloud books
real objects
rewards
role-playing
sand trays
simulations
small group projects
tactile flash cards
tape recorder
transparencies
videotapes
visualization techniques
wipe-off boards
writing experiences

Sample Classroom Contracts

Contracts can be effective tools for managing behavior, improving task completion, and for motivating positive school performance. When a contract is written, be sure to write a clear definition of what is expected of the child; the positive consequence for achieving the expectation, the negative consequence if the expectation is not met, what the student and adult involved is expected to do, and a plan for achieving the desired objectives. The following are two examples of contracts that are effective with younger children:

Weekly Contract for: _____

Goal: _____

Monday	Tuesday	Wednesday	Thursday	Friday

Reward: _____ **Dated:** _____

Signed: _____ **Signed:** _____
    (Student's name)   (Teacher's name)

- -

Contract for:_____	M	T	W	Th	F
Goal 1:					
Goal 2:					
Goal 3:					
Goal 4:					
Goal 5:					

Reward: _____ **Dated:** _____

Signed: _____ **Signed:** _____
    (Student's name)   (Teacher's name)

Activities to Motivate Struggling Readers

Struggling readers need a stimulating environment and activities that are interesting, engaging, and designed to help the child experience success. This can be accomplished by first interrupting the cycle of failure, or with very young children by not letting the cycle ever begin. Break down the lessons into manageable segments; provide children with assignment choices; incorporate their personal interests into lessons; and focus on progress. These activities will show children that reading can be fun and that they can also be successful readers!

Classroom Motivation and Management Activities and Tips

Fun Break

Plan frequent short breaks. Have the children get a drink, stand and stretch, or do a few exercises. Sing a song before starting the activity or play a quick game. Alternatively, vary the way the children return to their seats after reading. Play a short selection of music and let them march or race back to their chairs. Active young children will no longer get tired and restless from sitting for long periods.

Book Clubs

Organize a classroom book club. Membership is open to the whole class. Select a President to call the roll and a Secretary to record the book read at each meeting. Decide on a book-club name and make paper badges or hats with the club name on it that everyone can wear at the meetings. The members can vote on the book they want to read or have read to them. On the day of the meeting, the password to enter the club room may be the name of the book to be read that day. A discussion of the book and other related activities could follow. They could discuss illustrations, compare this book with others, suggest other books on the same subject, or pantomime the story. Clubs are simply excellent reading stimulators.

Reading Honor Roll Bulletin Board

Take a black and white close-up photograph of each child in the class. Place a caption on the bulletin board that says" We Are Honor Roll Readers." Every child's picture goes up on the bulletin board. The children will then get to earn stickers to be placed next to their photographs. To earn a sticker a child must keep a personal reading log. This reading log records the books that the child has read at home or books that the parents have read to the child. Set a goal that is appropriate for your class. Check reading logs weekly and then add the earned stickers to the bulletin board.

Book Exchange

Ask several other classes to join the fun! Prepare a presentation of some of your favorite stories. Each classroom takes a turn and presents their books. Then the classes can exchange the books. A later discussion between the classes about the books can be fun too!

Activities to Make Reading Exciting

Balloon Burst

Obtain a large balloon for each reading group and enough small balloons so that each child in the room gets one. Duplicate a short list of books to be read by each of the reading groups. Prepare enough copies so that each child gets one. Roll the lists into small enough balls to insert into the large balloon. Inflate the balloon and suspend it from the ceiling where the reading groups meet. Repeat this step for each reading group.

When each group comes to the reading circle, a child is selected to stick a pin in the balloon. When it pops, each child in the reading group scrambles for a copy of the list. Make a chart of the book titles. Each time a child reads one of the listed books, they should receive a small balloon.

The Reading Wagon

Bring a wagon into the classroom and let the children have the fun of decorating it. Then brainstorm with the children for the titles of their favorite books. Collect those titles and place them in the wagon. At reading or story time, a child is chosen to get the wagon and select a book. The wagon is also fun for independent reading time. One child can pull the wagon around the classroom, stopping and allowing each child to select a book.

The reading wagon can be extremely motivational if the teacher takes the time to fill the wagon with the children's favorite topics, favorite titles, or books about things that the children would like to learn more about. The wagon can also become a theme-wagon and be filled with books on different subjects or themes being studied at school.

Story Time Serial

(See pages 87–88 for a list of Great Read-Aloud Books)
Take a long story or a book and read a part of it out loud each day. Stop reading at a particularly exciting point in the story. Exclamations of disappointment will follow, but excitement will precede the next session. The whole idea is to leave the children wanting to hear more of the story. The children will hardly be able to wait for the book to be finished and placed on the library table for them to read.

To make this activity even more exciting, the teacher can add props as she reads the story. For example, if the story involves a princess, the teacher could wear a tiara. When the story involves a pirate, the teacher could bring in a toy parrot or wear an eye patch. If the story involves an animal, the teacher could display a similar stuffed animal in the classroom.

Sound Effects

Sound effects can add excitement to almost any story. Tape recordings can be made of rain, wind, and other weather conditions; the children can record cheering, booing, and laughing; and stories with repeated phrases can be recorded, such as "I'll huff and I'll puff and I'll blow your house down." Children will enjoy anticipating hearing the sound effects.

Special Places To Read

The Reading Cottage

Secure a large appliance box to be the cottage and cut out two large windows for light on each side and a front door large enough for a child to enter. Have the children paint the cottage a bright color. Add extra touches such as curtains, shutters, and artificial flowers. Place a comfortable chair inside. Attach a sign on the cottage that says, "QUIET! SOMEONE IS READING." The children will appreciate having a pleasant and secluded spot to enjoy books. Inexpensive cardboard reading carrels can also be decorated and turned into special reading places.

Big Special Reading Chair

Garage sales can sometimes provide some wonderful treasures for a classroom. An extra large overstuffed chair can be a comfortable and cozy place to read. Two small children can also fit nicely into one large chair. Paired reading is especially fun in a huge chair.

The Magic Reading Carpet

Spread a small rug on the floor near the library table. Call it the "magic reading carpet." Place several fairy tale books on the rug. A child can sit on this carpet and be transported to other times and other places. This is an enticing way to promote the reading of fairy tales or just the fun of reading books.

Library Corner in Your Classroom

Most classrooms have a special library corner. If possible, create the library corner near a bulletin board. Change the display frequently with rotating themes, such as horses, favorite authors, topics that the children want to learn about, or favorite stories of the children.

The children can design individual book covers about themselves. Place a caption above this bulletin-board display that says, "We Love to Read!"

Turn Reading into Art

New Book Advertisements

Design a billboard bulletin board that advertises new books. The children can make posters of their favorite books—books that they think other children would enjoy reading.

Jigsaw Puzzle

Paste old book covers onto heavy cardboard. Cut them into irregular pieces to make jigsaw puzzles. The pieces for each set can be kept in a labeled envelope or in an empty shoe box. After a child has assembled a puzzle, he just may be interested in reading the actual book.

Simple Bookmark

A simple kind of bookmark can be made by fitting a marker in hat fashion over the corner of a page. Copy the pattern at the bottom of this page onto construction paper. Cut out the shape, fold in half, and fold again on the dashed line. Then glue this flap where marked to the back of the bookmark. More durable bookmarks can be made out of felt.

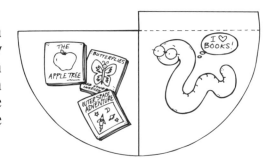

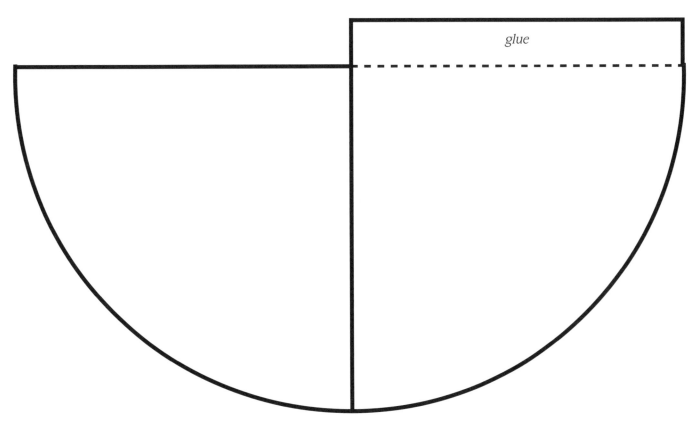

glue

Book Art

Use a book to stimulate an art project. Encourage the children to work with different mediums such as paint, charcoal, clay, or papier-mâché to illustrate a scene or to mold a character from the book. Let the beautiful art work found in books suggest an art project. For example, *The Snowy Day,* by Jack Ezra Keats could be used to create an original collage or *Swimmy* by Leo Lionni could be used to create watercolor prints. The pleasure found in books can be expressed through art.

Book Mobile

Have the children draw pictures of book characters, color them, and cut them out. Be sure to color both sides. Use a wire hanger and lightweight string to attach the cutouts. Suspend the mobile from the ceiling or a light fixture near a door or window. Allow the breeze to move the mobile and thus remind the children of the good books they have read.

Book Mural

Consider making a class mural for a great book enjoyed by the class. Discuss with the group what aspects of the book they would like to show and in what medium. Murals can be done on wrapping paper and a variety of effects can be achieved by using chalk, paint, and crayons. Give every child an assignment and a space on the mural on which to work. The mural will express the class spirit and creativity spurred by a book.

Multi-Sensory Reading and Writing Centers

Reading Learning Center

Set up three tables in a corner of the room. For each table, plan a reading station that will focus on a specific learning style. On the first table construct a manipulative lesson to introduce a skill, on the second table set up a game to practice a skill, and on the third table develop an activity to assess the skill. Label each station and provide simple directions for the tasks at each table. Game boards and any other needed materials should be kept on the tables.

For example, at the first learning station the teacher could have the tactile learning experience of molding sight-words from play dough or clay. The children are to mold the sight words *is*, *it*, and *in*. On the second table, the children could play the visual card game of memory matching—finding matches for the words *is*, *it*, and *in*. And finally, at the third learning station, the children could be given a short story with the words *is*, *it*, and *in* used frequently and a tape recording of the story. First, the children read through the sheet and circle the words and then they can listen to the story that has been recorded. As a fun extra activity, the children could make their own tape recording of the story. Multi-sensory learning centers can be a highly motivational alternative to traditional seat work.

Multi-Sensory Writing Center

A multi-sensory writing center has many more supplies than just paper and pencils. Here are some suggestions for easy-to-find materials that are great for a writing center. If possible, provide an old typewriter or a computer and allow the child to "type" words. Looking for letters and then typing them is a lot of fun for children. A cookie sheet filled with clean sand or salt is also a wonderful tool. The children can practice printing with their fingers. Finger paint with an added texture, such as salt, sand, or even coffee can be used. Adding scents to finger paint is also fun.

White glue with tempera paint added or glitter glue are wonderful for children to practice printing letters or for writing high-frequency words. When the glue is dry, the children can "feel" what they wrote.

Make up telegrams by cutting words out of newspapers or magazines. Paste the messages on blank paper. The children can read the messages to their friends. It is suggested that you clip words from advertisements because they generally have the largest type.

Make Reading Come Alive Through Drama

Book Chain

This is an alternative to a language experience story. Select three children to make up a story. The first child begins the story with a description of a character, the second child tells something interesting that happens to that character, and the third child tells how the story ends.

The teacher writes what the children have said on chart paper. These stories can also be recorded, duplicated, and distributed to each child in the class. Children love to read what they have imagined. This is also a great tool for teaching high-frequency words. These imaginative sequences can make for irresistible reading.

Puppet Plays

Make puppets of story characters and act out favorite stories from books or from a basal reading program. Simple and quick puppets can be made from construction paper, paper bags, or socks. Drawings of construction paper characters can be cut out and glued onto pencils, tongue depressors, or craft sticks. Construction paper features can be pasted onto the paper bags. Scraps of material for clothing, buttons for eyes, and yarn for hair and the mouth can transform a sock into a puppet.

A desk can be placed in front of the chalkboard to be used as the stage. Scenery can be drawn on cardboard and placed on the chalk tray. Construction paper can be used to make needed props, such as dishes and boats for the sock puppets to manipulate.

Keep a puppet stage and a collection of puppets in your room. They can be used for inventing original stories or as characters for a current book being read or a basal reader. A little imagination, a change of voice, some action, and the children will bring to life a story and add a new dimension to their reading.

Flannel Board Stories

After hearing a story, the children can make cutouts of the characters using construction paper. A small piece of sandpaper or self-stick Velcro™ attached to the back of the cutouts will make the characters adhere to the flannel board. The children can manipulate the characters on the flannel board as they retell the story.

Deficits in Phonological and Phonemic Awareness: Common Problems for Struggling Readers

Phonemic awareness is the ability to work with individual sounds (phonemes) in spoken words. This skill must be taught and developed before children learn to read. Each child needs to understand that spoken words are made up of sounds—and that by combining, blending, and separating those sounds new words can be created.

Phonemic awareness is the first true step in learning how to read and is the skill that children with reading disabilities have the most difficult time acquiring. Children who are unable to hear the phonemes in spoken words and cannot understand how a sequence of sounds form individual words will, in all likelihood, have a difficult time in equating specific sounds to the corresponding letters. Phonemic awareness instruction benefits all children; however, it may actually make the difference between reading success and failure for over 20% of the children.

Importance of Understanding Rhyme

Listen to Me—We Can Rhyme—You'll See (Songs and Games)
The concept of "rhyme" can be introduced to children as young as toddlers and early preschool. Playing rhyming games and singing rhyming songs help children learn to pay attention to the sounds in words.

1. **Clapping and Action Games:** Many songs and games include clapping, bouncing, and tossing balls or beanbags. For example, clap, clap, snap (say, "cat"), clap, clap, snap (say, "hat"), clap, clap, snap (say, "rat"), clap, clap, snap (say, "tat"). Real words are not important—what is important is that the spoken words rhyme with the other words.

2. **Rhyming Word Jump-Up:** The children walk around the classroom. The teacher says two words. When the children hear a pair of words that rhyme, they jump up!

3. **The Name Game:** Children think this game is very silly. The teacher looks at "Nate" and calls him "Tate." Then she may look at "Katie" and call her "Matie." Let the children have fun thinking of new rhyming names for each other.

Let Loose—Seuss and the Goose!
Mother Goose and Dr. Seuss probably never knew the impact their rhymes have played in teaching phonemic awareness. Besides simply enjoying the delightful rhymes of Dr. Seuss and Mother Goose, children can participate in specific activities that focus on rhyming patterns. (See Children's Books and Songs to Increase Phonemic Awareness on pages 36–37.)

1. **Fill in the Blank:** Pause at the end of a rhyming phrase and let the children fill in the missing word. For example, "Jack and Jill, went up the _____."

2. **New Words:** Generate other words that rhyme with the ones in the text (Jill, hill), such as pill, fill, dill, Bill.

3. **Clap:** Clap every time a rhyming word is heard.

4. **Illustrations:** Have the children illustrate pairs of rhyming words, such as *Jill* and *hill*. Point at the illustrations in the book that rhyme.

5. **Silly Rhymes:** Make a new silly rhyme, such as "Grumty, Bumty sat in the tree. Grumty, Bumty fell on his knee."

More Advanced Rhyme-Time

1. **Take the Train:** One child is the engineer and begins to walk around the room. He says a word, stops at a child, and then that child says a word the rhymes with the engineer's word. The two children walk in a line and stop at the next child. The game keeps going until everyone has joined the train.

2. **Rhyming Pairs Memory Match:** Lay out picture cards and look for pairs that rhyme. The children should say the words out loud as they look and listen for the rhyming matches.

3. **Parrot-Talk:** Parrots usually mimic what is said, but this "parrot" is confused. He never says the word he hears; instead, he always says a word that rhymes. Let the children take turns being the "parrot" and the "parrot's owner."

4. **Smile Face Lollipops:** Provide each child with a yellow construction paper smile face attached to a craft stick. The teacher says pairs of words. If the pair rhymes, the children hold up their smile faces.

5. **Wrong Word:** The teacher shows the children three or four pictures. The children must decide which picture card in the set does not rhyme with the others.

6. **Ideas for Older Children:** Keep activities age appropriate. Use raps, slogans, commercials, and T-shirt sayings for rhyming practice. Reproduce the T-shirt pattern on page 31 for the children. They can use this T-shirt to practice writing their own T-shirt sayings.

T-Shirt Pattern

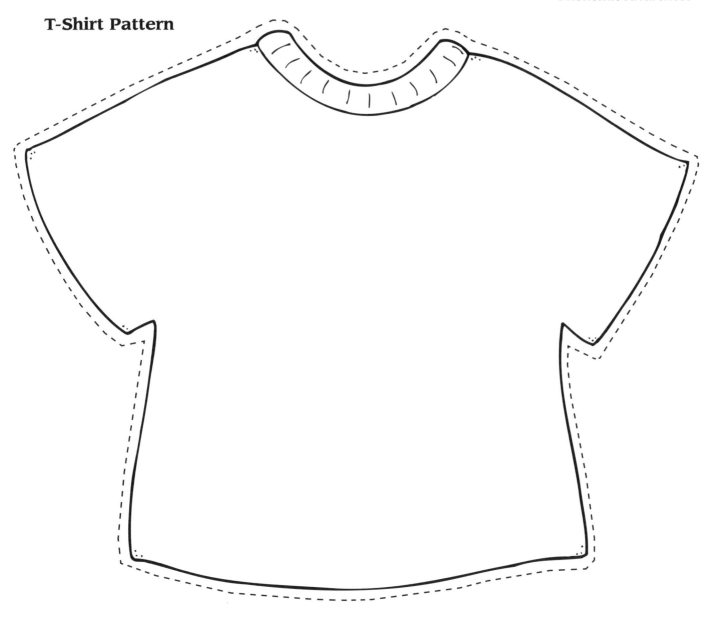

Teaching Syllable Segmentation

Teaching syllable segmentation is important because children must learn that words are comprised of multiple sounds.

1. **Syllable Clap:** Clapping out the number of syllables allows the children to really hear how words have multiple sounds. Children enjoy clapping out the syllables in their own names.

2. **Count 'em:** After the children clap each syllable, ask them how many syllables there were in the word. Write the number down.

3. **Syllable Surprise:** Fill a small bag with common classroom items. Let the children take turns picking an item out of the bag. Say the name of the item and then clap and count the syllables.

Phoneme Isolation and Identity

Emerging readers must also be able to recognize individual sounds in words (phoneme isolation) and be able to recognize the same sounds in different words (phoneme identity). It is advisable to first teach the sixteen consonants that have only one phoneme (b, d, f, h, j, k, l, m, n, p, q, r, t, v, x, z) and then introduce those letters that have more than one sound (c, g, s, w, y). Next add each vowel by introducing both of its sounds (long and short); and finally add the digraphs that each have two letters that create one sound (th, wh, ch, sh).

1. **Silly Sounds:** Introduce each phoneme with a sound association. For example, for /m/, teach the children the Campbell's Soup commercial—"mmmmmm good;" for /t/ use a metronome or ticking clock; or make a buzzing sound, "zzzzzzz" for /z/. Children will visualize the picture and it will help them remember the sound.

2. **Look in the Mirror:** Let children watch themselves as they say new sounds.

3. **Repeat Initial Sounds:** Isolating the first sound helps children understand sound placement. For example, say the word by "stretching" the sounds, p-p-p-p-p-pig; llllllll-amp; MMMMMM-ary. Isolating phonemes in the middle and ending positions is also recommended.

4. **Tongue Twisters:** Use tongue twisters that feature the specific phoneme that the children are learning. (Tongue twister books can be found in the list of Children's Books and Songs to Increase Phonemic Awareness on pages 36–37.)

5. **Listen Carefully:** While reading aloud, have the children listen carefully for specific phonemes. To assist, accentuate the phoneme that you want them to identify.

6. **I Spy:** The teacher says, "I spy something that begins with /j/." The children walk around the room and try to find items that begin with that phoneme.

7. **Real Objects:** Have the children say the names of real objects and decide what sounds are in which position: beginning, middle, or end.

8. **Where Is the Sound?:** To help children visualize the placement of the sounds, work with wooden blocks. Use the "B" or "1" block to represent the beginning sound. Use the "M" or "2" block to represent the middle sound, and use the "E" or "3" block for the ending sound. For example, ask the child, "Where is the /d/ in *dog*?" The child would then pick up the "B" or "1" block. "Where is the /g/ in *dog*?" The child would then pick up the "E" or "3" block.

9. **Sound Sorting:** Sort pictures according to beginning or ending sounds. (Picture cards can be found on pages 38–42.)

Phonemic Segmentation

Phonemic segmentation is when a word is broken down into its separate sounds (phonemes). This can be a very difficult task for children. Make it fun—add a story component to help the children gain understanding. For example, tell them the story "The Tortoise and the Hare." Discuss how fast hares can run and how slowly tortoises move. Let the children run fast like a hare and walk slowly like a tortoise. Remembering the tortoise and the hare will help the children with many of the following activities:

1. **Talking Fast and Slow:** Say a word fast, just like the hare would move. Then say the same word very slowly, just like the tortoise would move. Let the children practice saying words fast and slow. When talking like the tortoise, be sure to help the children articulate each phoneme in the word. Try counting the phonemes after the word is spoken slowly.

2. **Picture Train:** Use the patterns of the engine, train car, and caboose on page 34. Copy the patterns onto card stock, color, cut out, and place a self-stick magnet on the back of each train car. Each train car represents the placement of a phoneme. Initially use CVC words: *cat, dog, pig, hat, man, hen, red, bed, tin,* etc. Each of these words has a beginning, a middle, and an end—just like the train. After saying the complete word, move each train car as you say the individual phonemes. The children can see the train move and connect the individual sounds.

3. **Stretching Words:** Use a large rubber band to demonstrate how words can stretch. The teacher pulls the rubber band as she says a word. For example, the word "run" would be stretched as /rrrrrrrrrrrrrrrr/-/uuuuuuuuuu/-/nnnnnnnnn/.

4. **Connecting Blocks:** Use interlocking blocks to represent the sequential sounds in words. Demonstrate by "putting together" and "taking apart" the individual phonemes in selected words.

Deleting, Adding, and Substituting Phonemes

Children are now ready to gain experience with recognizing that when a phoneme is removed, added, or substituted a new word is created. For example, deleting the /b/ in *bread* changes the word to *read*. Adding /s/ to *pace* changes the word to *space*. Also, by substituting /h/ for /t/ changes *hen* to *ten*.

1. **Play Add-On and Take-Away:** Give children words and ask them to repeat the word minus a sound, or with an additional sound, such as take away the /k/ from *monkey* and now it is *money*, or add /l/ to *feet* to make the word *fleet*.

2. **Sing Songs:** Sing songs and change the phonemes in the chorus, such as in "Old MacDonald's," *ee-i-ee-i-o* to *mee-i-mee-i-to* or "The Farmer in the Dells'" chorus of *hi-ho-the-dario, the farmer in the dell*, to *di-do-the-mario, the charmer in the well*. Children will giggle as they think of funny new choruses for familiar songs.

Train Patterns

Finally, when children thoroughly understand the unique workings of phonemes, they will understand that the sequencing and then the blending of spoken phonemes creates words. For example, the phonemes /p//e//n/ are really parts of the spoken word *pen*.

1. **Surprise Bag:** Fill a bag with classroom objects. Pick an object out of the bag and say the name of the object just as the tortoise would—very slowly. The children respond like the hare and say the word quickly. Repeat in the reverse. The teacher says the word quickly and the children repeat the same word slowly.

2. **Guess What?:** The teacher says, "I am thinking of something. It is something you can eat. Guess what it is?" Then the teacher states the name of a food in a segmented fashion. The children respond quickly with the correct word.

3. **Onset and Rime:** Use the concept of onset and rimes. Give the children an onset, such as /g/ and the rime /-oat/. The children put it together and say "goat."

Here are some of the most common rimes: -at, -ag, -ay, -ack, -ank, -ang, -ake, -ail, -ap, -am, -an, -ain, -ell, -eed, -en, -est, -ed, -ew, -ed, -ill, -ip, -ick, -ing, -in, -ink, -ine, -ight, -im, -ot, -out, -op, -ow, -ore, -ob, -ock, -ug, -uck, -um, -un.

4. **Go Sliding:** Provide the children with an onset and then a rime before having them go down the slide. At the top of the slide the child says the onset and then the rime separately. When the child hits the bottom of the slide, he then says the whole word quickly.

Children's Books and Songs to Increase Phonemic Awareness

Books

10 in a Bed. Anne Geddes. (Andrews McMeel Publishing, 2001)
ABC I Like Me. Nancy Carlson. (Viking, 1997)
Altoona Baboona. Janie Bynum. (Harcourt, 1999)
Amelia Bedelia. Peggy Parish. (HarperTrophy, 1992)
Asana and the Animals: A Book of Pet Poems. Grace Nichols. (Candlewick Press, 1997)
Bear Snores On. Karma Wilson. (Margaret K. McElderry, 2002)
The Best Storybook Ever. Richard Scarry. (Golden Books, 2000)
The Biggest Tongue Twister Book in the World. Gyles Daubeney Brandreth. (Sterling Publishing, 1981)
Blue Bowl Down: An Applalachian Rhyme. C.M. Millen. (Candlewick Press, 2004)
Bowl Patrol. Marilyn Janovitz. (North South Books, 1996)
Bubble Gum, Bubble Gum. Lisa Wheeler. (Megan Tingley, 2004)
Bus Stop, Bus Go! Daniel Kirk. (Putnam, 2001)
Casey Jones. Allan Drummond. (Farrar, Straus, and Giroux, 2001)
The Cat Barked. Lydia Monks. (Dial Books, 1999)
Cat in the Hat. Dr. Seuss. (Random House, 1957)
Chugga-Chugga Choo-choo. Kevin Lewis. (Hyperion, 1999)
Clara Ann Cookie, Go To Bed! Harriet Ziefert. (Walter Lorraine Books, 2000)
Clever Crow. Cynthia DeFelice. (Atheneum, 1998)
Dinosaur Chase. Carolyn Otto. (HarperCollins, 1991)
Dinosaur Roar! Paul Stickland, Henrietta Stickland. (Dutton Books, 1997)
A Dragon in a Wagon. Lynley Dodd. (Gareth Stevens Publishing, 2000)
Dumpy LaRue. Elizabeth Winthrop. (Henry Holt and Co., 2004)
Edwina the Emu. Sheena Knowles. (HarperTrophy, 1997)
Faint Frogs Feeling Feverish: And other Terrifically Tantalizing Tongue Twisters. Lilian Obligado.
    (Puffin Books, 1996)
"Fire! Fire!" Said Mrs. McGuire. Bill Martin Jr. (Voyager Books, 1999)
Fox in Socks. Dr. Seuss. (Random House, 1965)
Frog Went a-Courtin'. John Langstaff. (Gulliver Books, 1955)
A Giraffe and a Half. Shel Silverstein. (HarperCollins, 1964)
Good Night Pillow Fight. Sally Cook. (Joanna Cotler, 2004)
Grandma's Cat. Helen Ketteman. (Houghton Mifflin, 1996)
Green Eggs and Ham. Dr. Seuss. (Random House, 1960)
Greetings, Sun. Phillis Gershator and David Gershator. (Dorling Kindersley, 1998)
The Happy Day. Ruth Krauss. (HarperCollins, 1949)
The Helen Oxenbury Nursery Story Book. Helen Oxenbury. (Knopf Books, 1985)
Henny Penny. Paul Galdone. (Clarion Books, 1979)
The Hokey Pokey. Larry La Prise. (Simon & Schuster, 1996)
Honk! Toot! Beep! Samantha Berger. (Cartwheel Books, 2001)
A House is a House for Me. Mary Ann Hoberman. (Viking, 1978)
How Big is a Pig? Clare Beaton. (Turtleback Books Distributed, 2003)
I Can Fly. Ruth Krauss. (Simon & Schuster, 1955)
I Love Trains! Philemon Sturges. (HarperCollins, 2001)
I Love You, Good Night. Jon Buller. (Simon & Schuster, 1988)
Inch by Inch: The Garden Song. David Mallett. (HarperTrophy, 1995)
I Saw the Sea and the Sea Saw Me. Megan Montague Cash. (Viking, 2001)
Is Your Mama a Llama? Deborah Guarino. (Scholastic, 1997)
Jesse Bear, What Will You Wear? Nancy White Carlstrom. (Simon & Schuster, 1986)
Llama Llama Red Pajama. Anna Dewdney. (Viking, 2005)
Louelle Mae, She's Run Away! Karen Beaumont Alarcon. (Henry Holt and Co., 1997)
Madeline. Ludwig Bemelmans. (Viking, 1958)
Messy Bessy. Pat McKissack and Frederick McKissack. (Children's Press, 1987)
Mice Twice. Joseph Low. (Aladdin, 1986)
Miss Spider Series. David Kirk, (Scholastic, 2000)
Mole in a Hole. Rita Golden Gelman. (Random House, 2000)
Mother Goose: A Collection of Classic Nursery Rhymes. Michael Hague. (Henry Holt, 1984)
Mrs. Brown Went to Town. Wong Herbert Yee. (Houghton Mifflin, 1996)

Mrs. McTats and her Houseful of Cats. Alyssa Satin Capucilli. (Margaret K. McElderry, 2001)
Mrs. Nosh and the Great Big Squash. Sarah Weeks. (Scholastic, 2001)
Mrs. Wishy Washy. Joy Cowley. (Philomel, 1999)
My Crayons Talk. Patricia Hubbard. (Henry Holt and Co., 1996)
My Grandma Lived in Gooligulch. Graeme Base. (Harry N. Abrams, 1990)
My Very First Mother Goose. Iona Archibald Opie. (Candlewick Press, 1996)
Nana's Hog. Larry Dane Brimner. (Children's Press, 1999)
Nathaniel Willy, Scared Silly. Judith Mathews. (Bradbury Press, 1994)
Nora's Room. Jessica Harper. (HarperCollins, 2001)
Pass the Peas, Please. Dina Anastasio. (Warner Books, 1990)
Pat-A-Cake and Other Play Rhymes. Joanna Cole and Stephanie Calmenson. (Morrow, 1992)
Pickles in My Soup. Mary Pearson. (Children's Press, 2000)
A Pinky Is a Baby Mouse and Other Baby Animals Names. Pam Munoz Ryan. (Hyperion, 1997)
A Place to Bloom. Lorianne Siomades. (Boyds Mills Press, 1997)
Play Rhymes. Marc Tolon Brown. (Puffin Books, 1993)
Poems to Read to the Very Young. Josette Frank. (Random House, 1988)
The Random House Book of Poetry for Children. Jack Prelutsky. (Random House, 1983)
Read-Aloud Rhymes for the Very Young. Jack Prelutsky. (Knopf Books, 1986)
Rub a Dub Dub. Kin Eagle. (Charlesbridge Publishing, 1999)
Scat, Cats. Joan Holub. (Puffin Books, 2001)
Shhhhh! Everybody's Sleeping. Julie Markes. (HarperCollins, 2005)
Sing a Song of Popcorn. Beatrice Schenk de Regniers. (Scholastic, 1988)
Six Sleepy Sheep. Jeffie Ross Gordon. (Boyds Mills Press, 1991)
Skunks. David T. Greenberg. (Megan Tingley, 2001)
Slinky Malinki. Lynley Dodd. (Tricycle Press, 2005)
Some Smug Slug. Pamela Duncan Edwards. (HarperCollins, 1996)
Splat. Mary Margaret Perez-Mercado. (Children's Press, 2000)
Stop that Noise! Paul Geraghty. (Knopf, 1993)
Surprises Collection. Lee Bennett Hopkins. (Harper & Row, 1984)
There Was an Old Witch. Howard Reeves. (Hyperion, 2000)
There's a Wocket in My Pocket. Dr. Seuss. (Random House, 1974)
The Three Wishes. Judith Bauer Stamper. (Cartwheel Books, 1998)
Time of Wonder. Robert McCloskey. (Viking Books, 1957)
Tiny Tim Collection. Jill Bennett. (Delacorte Press, 1982)
Tomie de Paola's Mother Goose. Tomie dePaola. (Putnam, 1985)
Top Cat. Lois Ehlert. (Harcourt, 1998)
Truck Talk: Rhyme on Wheels. Bobbi Katz. (Cartwheel Books, 1997)
Uno, Dos, Tres = One, Two, Three. Pat Mora. (Clarion Books, 1996)
Watch William Walk. Ann Jonas. (Greenwillow, 1997)
When the Dark Comes Dancing: A Bedtime Poetry Book. Nancy Larrick. (Putnam, 1983)
Where the Sidewalk Ends. Shel Silverstein. (HarperCollins, 1974)
Where the Wild Things Are. Maurice Sendak. (HarperCollins, 1988)
Which Witch is Which? Judi Barrett. (Atheneum, 2001)
Who is Tapping at My Window? A. G. Deming. (Dutton Books, 1988)
Wiggle. Doreen Cronin. (Atheneum, 2005)

Songs
American Folk, Game & Activity Songs. Pete Seeger. (Smithsonian Folkways, 2000)
American Folk Songs for Children. Mike Seeger and Peggy Seeger. (Rounder Select, 1997)
Children's Favorite Songs. Walt Disney Records. (Disney, 1991)
A Child's Celebration of Songs. Music for Little People. (Music Little People, 1992)
Little White Duck. Burl Ives. (Sony Wonder, 1991)
Muppet Hits. The Muppets. (Zoom Express, 1993)
Old Mr. Mackle Hackle. Gunnar Madsen. (G-Spot, 1999)
Peter, Paul and Mommy. Peter, Paul, and Mary. (Warner Bros, 1990)
Raffi Singable Songs Collection. Raffi. (Rounder, 1996)
Really Silly Songs About Animals. Bethie. (Discovery House Music, 1993)
Songs to Grow On For Mother and Child. Woody Guthrie. (Smithsonian Folkways, 1992)
You Sing a Song and I'll Sing a Song. Ella Jenkins. (Smithsonian Folkways, 1992)

Phonemic Awareness Picture Cards

The phonemic picture cards can be used for a variety of purposes. The cards can be matched according to rhyme (e.g., jar, car), beginning sounds, ending sounds, or the number of syllables in each word.

As children progress, the picture cards can be placed in groups of three to form words, such as the "cake" card, the "ant" card, and the "top" card—the three beginning phonemes would make the word *cat*.

Turning Words into Mental Images

A child with dyslexia primarily thinks in pictures rather than words. This type of learner needs to create mental images for words before being able to read them in print. These young readers may have a clear understanding of simple nouns, such as cat, dog, house, or mom, because it is easy to see a clear mental image of these things. Other words, such as most of the high-frequency words, (for example, *it*, *is*, *and*, *the*, and *was*) are far more difficult for these children because there are no mental pictures to accompany these words.

There are many fun activities, methods, and techniques that can assist children in developing the skill of mentally turning words into pictures. Although these techniques were designed for children with reading disabilities, they are also effective strategies for helping children who are not fluent readers.

Visualization of Pictures without Text

Children think of this activity as a game and have loads of fun. Use photographs or full-color illustrations of complicated pictures. Locate pictures in magazines, newspapers, story books, or even family photos. This activity not only helps children to learn to visualize mental images, but it also helps children learn how to listen.

Step 1: Do not show the children the picture you have chosen. Keep it hidden. Tell them you are going to play 20 (or more) questions that can only be answered with "yes" or "no." The children ask questions about the picture without seeing it. For example, "Are there people in the picture?" If yes, "Was the person a man or a woman?" "Was the picture taken outside?" "Are there trees in the picture?" The longer the children play, the more skillful they will become at asking questions.

Step 2: When you are satisfied that the children have asked enough questions about the picture, direct them to take out a piece of paper and crayons. Encourage the children to draw and color what they think the hidden picture looks like. Ask everyone to share their drawings when they are done.

Step 3: When the children are finished with their drawings, share the actual picture and let them compare the similarities and differences. If possible, make a color transparency of the picture and show it to the children using an overhead projector. This will make it easier for the children to compare the similarities and differences between the pictures.

Step 4: When the children have gained an understanding of this process, allow them to take turns being the person who gets to hold the hidden picture and answer everyone's questions.

To get you started: A reproducible visualization picture has been included on page 44. Copy and color the picture. Turn it into a color transparency.

Activities to Help Children
Learn How to Turn Words into Mental Images

Illustrations for Simple Sentences

An easy technique for increasing visualization skills is to have the children illustrate the meaning of simple sentences. This technique can be used with the stories from the classroom's basal reading program, a story the children might be reading together, or with sentences dictated by the children. Reproduce page 46 to get the children started using the illustration of simple sentences to increase visualization skills.

Comic Books

Cut out short comic strips from the daily paper. Select comics with simple vocabulary and humor that the children can understand, such as "Peanuts." First, cover up the text so the children can only look at the pictures. Discuss what is happening in each vignette, and have the children guess what might be funny about the cartoon.

Then show the children the words. Read it together. The cartoon can be spontaneously acted out and the whole class can laugh together. Discuss if their guess was correct about what they thought might be funny in the comic. Keep a collection of the comic strips and attach them to pieces of card stock. Combine the pages into a classroom comic book that the children can read and chuckle over again and again!

Copycat

Have the children in the reading group share the experiences of the characters following reading a story in the basal reader. For example, if a boat is featured in a story, have the children make construction paper boats. If there's a race in a story, have the children engage in a similar race. If the children eat cookies in the story, give each child a cookie. If a song is sung in the story, have the children sing it. Children will love sharing experiences with the story book characters.

This exercise can also be a wonderful activity for specific selected vocabulary chosen by the teacher. Use words that the children find difficult to read and where a visual and tactile experience would provide added reading support.

Treasure Chest Book Adventures

Give each child an envelope. Inside the envelope is a piece of paper with a couple of pictures that have something to do with the selected story. Have the children find the picture clues as they read the story. This task will help children learn to focus on details while engaging them with a fun reason to "hunt" through the story. It also provides visual story clues which can be used to stimulate the children's prior knowledge and meaning before they begin reading the story.

Name _____

Illustrate the Sentences
Read, draw, and read again.

My mom made me lunch.	The little boy fell out of bed.
My friend got a new doll.	I went outside to play with the dog.

Sorting Words

Teach children that words can be sorted in many different ways. Some words represent people or animals; some words are places, like the library or a kitchen; some words are things, like toys or school tools; some words are actions, like running or swimming; and some words are descriptive, such as sizes, colors, and shapes.

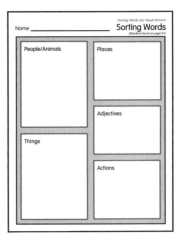

By using words on flash cards with pictures, the children can sort new story vocabulary words on the chalk rails or by using a pocket chart. Children can also draw pictures of these news words.

On page 48 is a reproducible graphic organizer that children can use to illustrate and sort vocabulary. For example, in the story of "The Three Pigs," the children might draw pictures of a pig and a wolf in the "People/Animals" box; a forest in the "Places" box; brick, sticks, and straw in the "Things" box; the wolf blowing or the pigs running in the "Actions" box; and pink pigs or a furry wolf in the "Adjectives" box.

Clay—High-Frequency Words

Play dough or modeling clay is probably the best tactile material that children with reading disabilities can use. Clay can be used to model individual letters and to create high-frequency words.

For children who need to have visual images of words, a clay model can serve as that visual model. Here is an example, provide the children with a variety of pictures that represent nouns and three molded clay letters of the word *and*. The children lay out a picture card (cat), the clay word *and*, as well as another picture card (dog). The children practice reading, "cat and dog." Using clay to teach words that do not have a visual picture can significantly increase a child's word recognition skills of sight words and of high-frequency words.

A Picture Is Worth a Thousand Words

Books that have no words, just lovely illustrations, can provide wonderful early literacy and visual learning experiences. Sit with the children and let them put their own words to the story. Creating their own stories stimulates imagination and increases language skills.

As the children progress and begin to actually read some words, let them create their own books. Cut out pictures from magazines and old "wordless" coloring books and then instruct the children to write sentences that go with their pictures. Children can also have great fun cutting words out of newspapers and magazines and arranging them into short sentences. Glue the words in proper sequence under each illustration.

Turning Words into Mental Images

Sorting Words

(Directions found on page 47.)

People/Animals

Places

Adjectives

Things

Actions

Sell-A-Word Poster

Have the children make a poster, banner, or sign to advertise a certain word. The word may be selected by either the child or the teacher. The ad must show the meaning of the word.

A fun variation: Posters can be made in which the key word is omitted. The children can try to guess what word is being sold.

Read and Draw Stories

Duplicate a simple story that the children can read aloud at the same time the story is being illustrated on the chalkboard by the teacher. This will make reading an exciting visual experience for every reader.

Rebus Stories

Copy the rebus stories found on pages 50 and 51 and the rebus pictures below. Have the children color and cut out the rebus pictures and then decide where the pictures should be placed in the story. The children can glue the pictures on the boxes once they have decided how they want their stories to read.

Reproducible rebus pictures to be used on story pages 50 and 51.

The Insects Had a Party

One day the ⬜ and the

⬜ went to a party.

They ate ⬜ and ⬜ .

They drank ⬜ . They got

to take ⬜ home. It was fun!

The Circus Comes to Town!

The circus is here! There are ☐ and ☐. The ☐ and ☐ are funny! The ☐ are loud. I like the ☐ best. I can eat ☐ and ☐. I went in the ☐. It was fun!

Marginalia

The actual definition of marginalia is "marginal notes," or "writing notes in the margins." This simply means that one writes notes or draws pictures in the margins of printed text. This is an old technique of study that has been used for hundreds of years. It is also an effective tool for children who need visual clues and who find note-taking to be helpful.

Younger children can be taught to analyze text and draw pictures that will help them remember the words and understand the meaning of the story. As children grow older and become more capable readers, they can be taught to write notes and questions about the text. For many years educators have known the value of note-taking for all learners, especially for aiding struggling readers.

The following story is an example of how young children can be taught to use the margins of a text.

Today is Maria's birthday and the day of her surprise party. The party was suppose to be a secret, but her good friend Juan let the secret slip. Maria's mother had asked Juan to help plan the party. Juan was happy to help and was filled with all sorts of good ideas.

Juan knew how much Maria loved horses, so he bought her a special pony piñata. He filled the piñata with Maria's favorite candy, bubble gum, milk chocolate and lemon drops. Juan also bought Maria the necklace she had seen in the store window.

It was going to be a great party. But everything changed yesterday! Maria looked at Juan and said, "Why are you so happy?"

Juan blurted out, "Because tomorrow you are going to have the best surprise birthday party!" Maria promised to act surprised!

Books Without Words

Alligator's Toothache. Diane De Groat. (Random House, 1977)
Alphabet in Nature. Judy Feldman. (Children's Press, 1991)
The Angel and the Soldier Boy. Peter Collington. (Knopf Books, 1991)
Animal Alphabet. Bert Kitchen. (Puffin Books, 1988)
Anno's Counting Book. Anno Mitsumasa. (HarperTrophy, 1986)
Anno's Flea Market. Anno Mitsumasa. (Philomel, 1984)
Anno's Journey. Anno Mitsumasa. (Sagebrush, 1999)
April Fools. Fernado Krahn. (Dutton Books, 1974)
Big Ones, Little Ones. Tana Hoban. (William Morrow, 1976)
Breakfast for Jack. Pat Schories. (Front Street, 2004)
A Boy, a Dog, a Frog, and a Friend. Mercer Meyer. (Penguin Books, 1967)
Carl Goes Shopping. Alexandra Day. (Farrar, Straus, and Grioux, 1989)
Carl's Birthday. Alexandra Day. (Farrar, Straus, and Grioux, 1997)
Carl's Christmas. Alexandra Day. (Farrar, Straus, and Grioux, 1990)
Changes, Changes. Pat Hutchins. (Aladdin, 1987)
Creepy Castle. John Goodall. (Atheneum Books, 1991)
The Creepy Thing. Fernado Krahn. (Houghton Mifflin, 1982)

Do You Want to Be My Friend? Eric Carl. (Philomel, 1988)
Find Waldo Now. Martin Hanford. (Little Brown, 1988)
First Snow. Emily Arnold McCully (Trophy Press, 1988)
Flying Jake. Lane Smith. (Aladdin, 1996)
Frog Goes to Dinner. Mercer Meyer. (Penguin Books, 1974)
Frog, Where Are You? Mercer Meyer. (Penguin Books, 1969)
Full Moon Soup: A Wordless Book That's Brimful of Stories. Alistair Graham. (Kingfisher, 1991)
Good Dog, Carl. Alexandra Day. (Scholastic, 1985)
The Grey Lady and the Strawberry Snatcher. Molly Bang. (Simon & Schuster, 1984)
Hiccup. Mercer Meyer. (Penguin Books, 1978)
The Hunter and the Animals. Tomie de Paola. (Holiday House, 1981)
I Read Signs. Tana Hoban (HarperTrophy, 1987)
I Read Symbols. Tana Hoban (Greenwillow, 1983)
Is It Red? Is It Blue? Tana Hoban (Sagebrush, 1999)
Jack and the Missing Piece. Pat Schories. (Front Street, 2004)
Look Book. Tana Hoban (Greenwillow, 1997)
Looking Down. Steve Jenkins. (Houghton Mifflin, 2003)
Moonlight. Jan Ormerod. (Frances Lincoln, 2004)
Noah's Ark. Peter Spier. (Double Day Books, 1977)
On Christmas Eve. Peter Collington. (Knopf Books, 1990)
Paddy Pork's Holiday. John Goodall. (Atheneum Books, 1976)
Pancakes for Breakfast. Tomi de Paola. (Harcourt, 1978)
The Paperboy. Dav Pilkey. (Scholastic, 1996)
People. Peter Spier. (Double Day Books, 1980)
Picnic. Emily Arnold McCully. (HarperCollins, 2003)
The Red Book. Barbara Lehman. (Houghton Mifflin, 2004)
Rosie's Walk. Pat Hutchins. (Simon & Schuster, 1968)
The Secret in The Dungeon. Fernado Krahn. (Houghton Mifflin, 1983)
Shapes in Nature. Judy Feldman. (Children's Press, 1991)
Sidewalk Circus. Paul Fleischman and Kevin Hawkes. (Candlewick, 2004)
Sing Pierrot Sing. Tomie de Paola. (Harcourt, 1983)
Skates! Ezra Jack Keats. (Simon & Schuster, 1981)
The Snowman. Raymond Biggs. (Random House, 1978)
The Surprise Picnic. John Goodall. (McElderry, 1999)
Time Flies. Eric Rohmann (Crown Books, 1994)
Up a Tree. Ed Young. (HarperCollins, 2004)
The Tunnel Calamity. Edward Gorev. (Putnam, 1984)
Where's Waldo. Martin Hanford. (Candlewick, 1997)
Wills' Mammoth. Rafe Martin. (G.P. Putnam's Sons, 1989)
Window. Jeannie Baker. (Greenwillow, 1981)
The Yellow Umbrella. Henrik Drescher. (Kane/Miller Publishers, 2002)
Zoom. Istavan Banyai. (Viking Books, 1995)

Interventions for Correcting Reversals and Inversions: Letters, Numbers, and Words

It is not unusual for young children who are just learning how to hold a pencil and how to print, to reverse or invert some letters and numbers. In fact, backward writing and reversals of letters and small words are actually common in the early stages of handwriting development. Simply because a child reverses some letters does not mean that the child has dyslexia or will even have a difficult time learning to read. There need to be other signs to determine if a child is at risk for reading disabilities.

It is also equally important to mention that children who have dyslexia or other related reading disabilities do not necessarily reverse or invert letters, numbers, or words. Unfortunately, so many people have believed that reversals are part of the problems of dyslexia that many children with reading disabilities have not been diagnosed because they print accurately.

As young children mature, the reversals and inverted letters should begin to correct themselves. If not, there are intervention techniques that can help correct those errors.

Understanding Left from Right

One of the major keys in correcting reversals and inversions is a solid understanding of the concepts of "left" and "right." The following ideas and reproducible activities (pages 55–58) will provide the help children need to learn left from right.

Left and Right Bracelets
Let each of the children make construction paper bracelets, decorated with letter reminders of "L" on the left-handed bracelet and reminders of "R" on the right-handed bracelet. Another idea is for children to wear a bracelet only on the hand that they automatically write with.

Perfume or Cologne Fun
After children are beginning to understand the concepts of left and right, sometimes a tiny bit of perfume or cologne on only one wrist can be a helpful reminder. You can put a LOVELY smell on the LEFT wrist or a REALLY NICE smell on the RIGHT wrist. Note: Check for allergies before using fragrances in the classroom.

Reproducible Pages
Use the "Left Hand — Right Hand" activity on page 55; "Lefty, the Lucky Clown" on page 56; and "Rolly, The Right-Handed Rabbit" on page 57 as the children are ready.

Name: _____

Right Hand

Left Hand

Right Directions: Draw a ring on the right hand.
Trace the word "right" on the bracelet.

Left Directions: Trace the "L" on the left hand.
Trace the word "left" on the bracelet.

Name _____

Lefty, the Lucky Clown

Directions read by teacher:

1. Color the balloon in Lefty's left hand.
2. Color the heart on Lefty's left side.
3. Color Lefty's left shoe.
4. Circle Lefty's left patch.
5. Color the bird on Lefty's left shoe.
6. Draw an "L" on Lefty's left hand.

Name _____

Rolly, the Right-Handed Rabbit

Directions read by teacher:

1. Draw and color some flowers in Rolly's right hand.
2. Draw and color a bracelet on Rolly's right arm.
3. Draw and color a shoe on Rolly's right foot.
4. Print an "R" on Rolly's right ear.
5. Draw and color a ribbon on Rolly's right ear.
6. Color the basket in Rolly's right hand.

——— **Activities to Correct the Most Common Reversals and Inversions** ———

Desk Tapes

Individual student alphabet-line desk tapes can prove to be helpful reminders for children who may still be reversing letters. You may decide to make your own or purchase commercially-made desk tapes. On purchased desk tapes, have the children color the enclosed circular spaces on the letters and numbers. For example, color in the ball area on the lowercase b. This provides additional clues which help the children see the correct formation of each letter or number. A reproducible desk tape has been included for your convenience. Sometimes, it is only necessary to copy and tape to a desk the letters and numbers that the child routinely reverses or inverts.

A B C D E F G H I
J K L M N O P Q R
S T U V W X Y Z a
b c d e f g h i j
k l m n o p q r s
t u v w x y z 0 1
2 3 4 5 6 7 8 9 10

Practice Printing with Tactile Experiences

Daily practice using a variety of materials will help correct reversals.

Chalkboards

Have the child spend a few minutes every day writing the letters that are causing problems on the chalkboard. The child can practice making them large to really "feel" the direction of the letters. The child should say the name of the letter each time it is written on the board. Large movements seem to help children internalize the directionality of the letters.

Finger Paint Fun

Let children practice printing letters and numbers with finger paints that not only utilize the sense of touch and sight, but also can involve the senses of smell and taste. The more senses that children can stimulate as they reinforce proper directionality, the faster they may correct the reversals and inversions.

Minty Finger Paint

You will need: wallpaper paste or wheat paste (be sure it is safe for the children to use), water, food coloring, oil of wintergreen, large mixing bowl, spoon or other utensil for stirring, and finger paint paper

What you do: Mix the wallpaper paste or wheat paste with water until you have a thin paste. Add the food coloring and a few drops of oil of wintergreen. For more fun, try adding other scents such as vanilla, peppermint, lemon, or almond.

Clove-Scented Finger Paint

You will need: 1 cup (240 mL) sugar, food coloring, 2 cups (470 mL) flour, pan, 2 cups (470 mL) cold water, large mixing bowl, 6 cups (1.4 L) boiling water, spoon or other utensil for stirring, 1 tablespoon (15 mL) boric acid, finger paint paper, and oil of cloves

What you do: Mix the flour and cold water together. Add the sugar and stir until smooth. Add the flour, cold water, and sugar mixture to the boiling water, stirring constantly until thick. Remove from the heat and add the boric acid and several drops of the oil of cloves. Stir in the food coloring and then store the paint in a sealed container.

Textured Gritty Finger Paint

You will need: 1 cup (240 mL) flour, 1 cup (240 mL) water, food coloring, 1 to 1-1/2 cups (240–360 mL) of salt or sand, large mixing bowl, spoon or another utensil for stirring, finger paint paper

What you do: Combine the flour with the salt or sand. Add the water and stir until thoroughly mixed. Add the food coloring, one drop at a time, until you achieve the desired color.

Edible Gelatin Finger Paint

You will need: flavored gelatin, 9" x 13" (23 cm x 33 cm) pan, mixing bowl, spoon, and finger paint paper

What you do: Mix the gelatin according to the package directions. Place the gelatin in the refrigerator until it is a "gooey" consistency! Now use the gelatin to finger paint. It's icky–sticky hilarious fun!

Name

"b" and "d"

1. When you need to remember which way "b" faces and which way "d" faces, just think about the two letters as "good friends." Say the first four letters of the alphabet: a, b, c, d; "b" comes first and faces "d."

2. Place your hands, palms down on a table. Spread your pointer fingers and thumbs far apart. Visualize a "b" fitting inside your left hand. Visualize a "d" fitting inside your right hand.

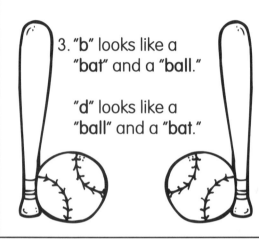

3. "b" looks like a "bat" and a "ball."

   "d" looks like a "ball" and a "bat."

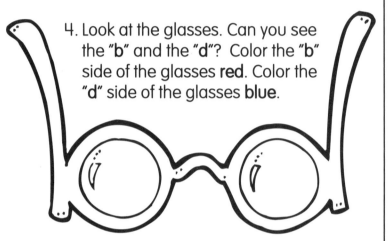

4. Look at the glasses. Can you see the "b" and the "d"? Color the "b" side of the glasses **red**. Color the "d" side of the glasses **blue**.

Trace each letter with a crayon.

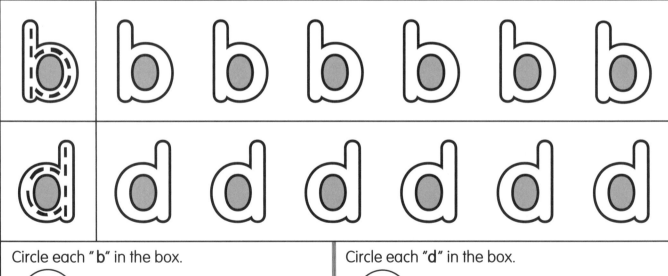

Circle each "b" in the box.

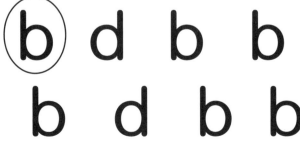

Circle each "d" in the box.

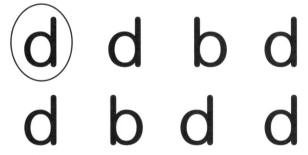

Name _____

"p" and "q"

p Porcupine begins with "p." The porcupine is looking for his quills.

Quills begins with "q." The quills protect the porcupine. q

1. Remember when you learned that "b" faces "d"—well, "p" faces "q" too! Just say the alphabet and you will see that "p" comes before "q."

2. Place your hands, palms up, and have your little fingers touching. Visualize the "p" hanging over the end of your left thumb. Now visualize a "q" hanging over your right thumb.

Trace each letter with a crayon.

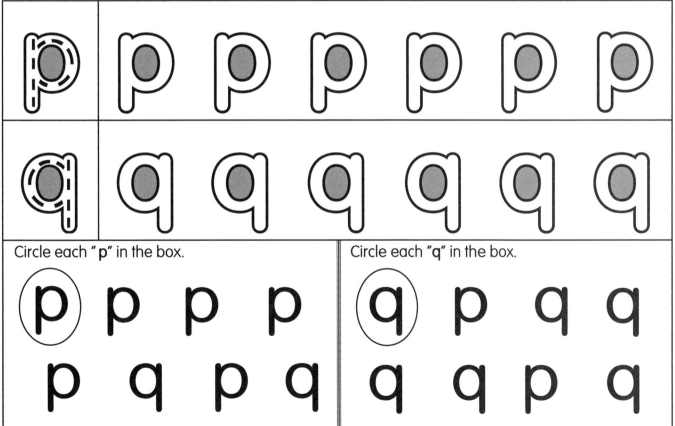

Circle each "p" in the box.

Circle each "q" in the box.

Name

"M" and "W"

The **M**en are **M**arching up and down the **M**ountain.

"**W**" is for **W**orm. I **W**onder **W**hy a **W**orm **W**iggles?

Trace each letter with a crayon.

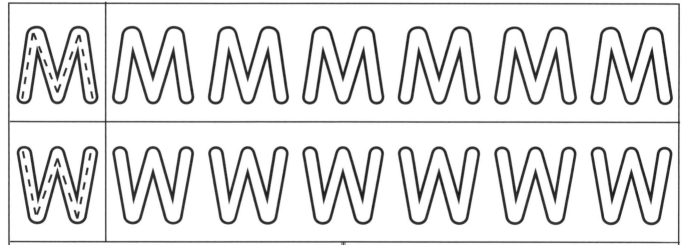

Circle each "M" in the box.

Circle each "W" in the box.

Name _____

"n" and "U"

"n" looks like a frow**n**.

"U" looks like a smile.

"n" looks like a **n**ose.

"U" looks like a c**U**p.

Trace each letter with a crayon.

Circle each "n" in the box.

Circle each "u" in the box.

Name _____

"S" or "s"

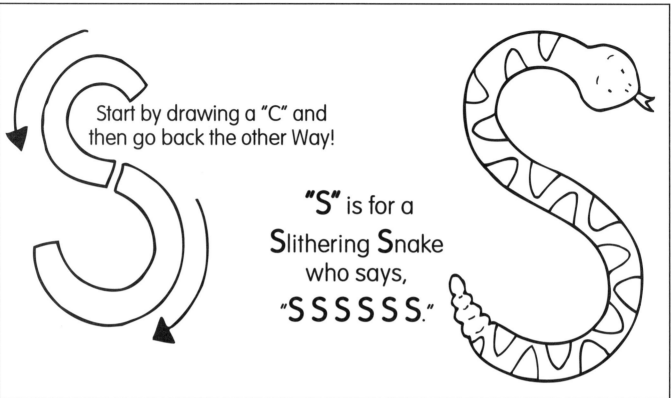

Start by drawing a "C" and then go back the other Way!

"S" is for a
Slithering **S**nake
who says,
"**SSSSSS**."

Trace each letter with a crayon.

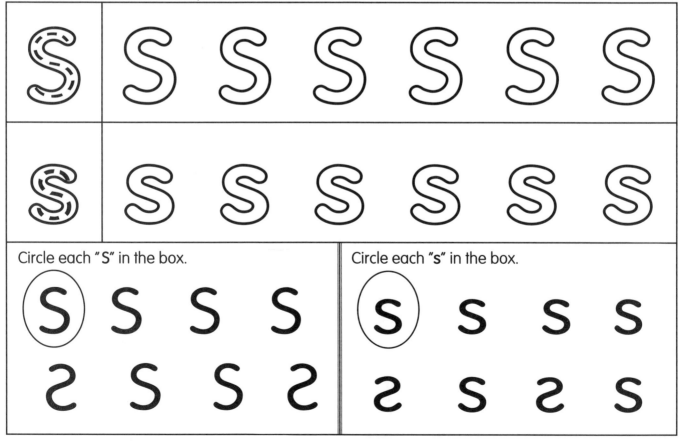

Circle each "S" in the box.

Circle each "s" in the box.

The Value of Graphic Organizers

Graphic organizers are excellent tools for children who need visuals to help them organize their thinking and to understand information.

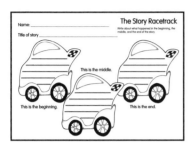

The Story Racetrack

This is a wonderful graphic organizer for helping children understand the beginning, the middle, and the end of a story. This activity can be found on page 69.

The children can also simply fold a large piece of paper into thirds. The sections are labeled beginning, middle, and end. The children can draw a picture that shows something that happened at these points in the story, or they can write and draw something that happened.

Story Pyramid

This activity can be done individually, in small groups, or as a large group. The reproducible activity can be found on page 70.

The pyramid is organized as follows:

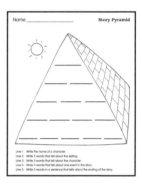

1. Write the name of character.
2. Write two words that tell about the setting.
3. Write three words that tell about a character.
4. Write four words in a sentence that tell about one event.
5. Write five words in a sentence that tells the ending of the story.

The Who, What, When, Where, and Why Reporter

Children benefit from the graphic organizer on page 71 that can help them answer the following questions, just like a newspaper reporter:

1. Who was in the story?
2. What happened?
3. When did it happen?
4. Where did it happen?
5. Why did it happen?

Star Maps

The Star Map reproducible graphic organizer on page 72 is one of the most versatile organizers. For example, it can be used for describing one of the characters in the story. To complete the organizer, have the child write the character's name in the center of the star and then write descriptive words about the character in the points of the stars. It can also be used to describe the main idea of the story. Write the main idea in the center of the star and the supporting details in the star points. Children also really enjoy the outer space theme of this graphic organizer.

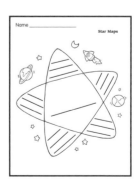

Cute Kid Character Map

When it is appropriate for the children to analyze a fictional character's personality traits, have them complete the Cute Kid Character Map on page 73. Using the graphic organizer as a prompt, direct the children to write the name of the character on the baseball cap and then fill in each body section with a few short words or phrases that describe the character's personality.

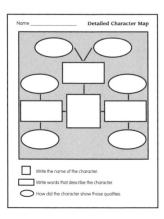

Detailed Character Map

To deepen a child's comprehension of a story, have the child analyze the main character and the main events that occurred. Using a copy of the Detailed Character Map on page 74, have each child list three of the character's personality traits in the rectangular boxes. Have them justify their decisions by identifying the character's actions, ideas, words, and feelings that support those chosen traits. The children can record that specific information in the oval shapes.

Comic Talk

The Comic Talk graphic organizer on page 75 can be used in a number of ways:

1. The two characters from the story can have a conversation by retelling the story.
2. The two characters from the story can have a conversation about something that could have happened in the story.
3. One character can pretend that he is conversing with one of the characters from another story.
4. This graphic organizer can also help compare different types of statements. The children can write a conversation between two characters about a predetermined topic. Have the first character always make factual statements and have the other character always answer with an opinion.

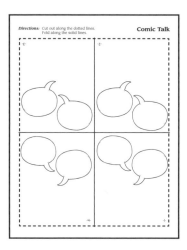

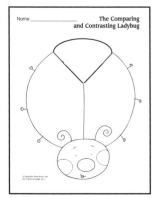

The Comparing and Contrasting Ladybug

To help the children identify similarities and differences in fictional characters, cultures, science topics and so on, provide a copy of The Comparing and Contrasting Ladybug on page 76. Use as a prompt to clarify their thinking. On the ladybug's wings the children can write the name of the topic and explain how each subject differs. In the section at the bottom of the ladybug, each child can list words that tell how the subjects are similar.

Venn Diagram

A Venn diagram can be two or three overlapping circles that are used for showing relationships between stories, fictional characters, science topics, sets of numbers, and other subjects. This is another effective comprehension tool for children to use when categorizing information. To complete the graphic organizer on page 77, identify the two topics being compared by writing each name above one of the circles and then list the description in the corresponding circle. Any details that are common to both topics would be recorded in the center of the diagram.

Here are some specific ideas for using the Venn diagram for analyzing information about a story. It can be used to compare:

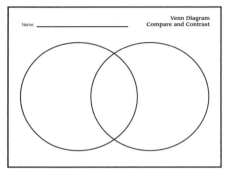

1. Two characters from the same story.
2. Two characters that are similar from two different stories.
3. Plots from two different stories.
4. Settings from two different stories.

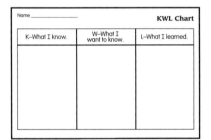

KWL Chart

The KWL chart on page 78 is the perfect tool for recalling prior knowledge and for helping students comprehend what they have read when working with nonfiction books or articles. Before the children read the selected text, encourage them to recall what they already know about the topic and record those comments in the column, "What I Know."

Next have the children talk about what they would like to learn about the topic, or think they will learn from the text, and then write those responses in the column "What I Want To Know."

Finally, after the children have read the text, encourage them to record any new specific information in the third column on the chart, "What I learned."

Storyboard

As the children read more complex stories, it is helpful for them to identify the main events. A simple storyboard, like the one on page 78, is an effective tool for organizing the events of a story in sequential order. Have the children write phrases or draw pictures to complete the storyboard.

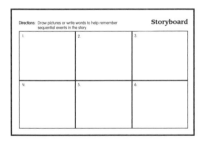

Main Idea Ice Cream Cone

This visual graphic organizer on page 79 certainly provides a "cool" way to organize details about a topic. After the children have read an informational article, discuss the main idea and the supporting points made by the author. Using a copy of the Main Idea Ice Cream Cone, each child should fill in the cone with the main idea and then write down the supporting details in the scoops of the ice cream.

Tic-Tac-Toe Notes

To help children focus on facts that are presented in text, have them complete the graphic organizer Tic-Tac-Toe Notes on page 80. When the chart is filled in, they will have identified nine major facts about the designated topic.

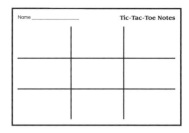

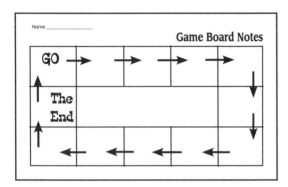

Game Board Notes

The graphic organizer on page 80 is meant to be used as the children are reading a selection. They can take notes or draw pictures in each section of the game board that describe the events in the story. This helps children to better organize and understand the sequence of a story.

My To Do List

For those children who have trouble remembering to complete tasks, the My To Do List on page 81 is a handy tool for organizing those pieces of information. Spelling lists and math facts can also be recorded on this simple chart for students to use while studying. This is the perfect tool for those children who can only handle short reminders for specific tasks.

My Weekly Assignment Planner

My Weekly Assignment Planner on page 81 provides children with a tool that will help them organize and remember all of the tasks that they need to accomplish during a week. The children can write down their assignments and other things that they need to remember to bring to school (or bring home). When the task is complete, the children can place a check-mark in the triangular box.

Word Organizer

A word organizer is a great tool for children who easily lose their place, skip lines, re-read lines, or omit words when reading text. A word organizer can be something as simple as a bookmark. Moving a bookmark as you read is helpful for distractible and inattentive students. It causes them to focus and pay attention to the page. The bookmarks are the most effective when they are 6 in. (15 cm) in length and about 1 in. (25 mm) wide. Draw a dark line about 1 in. (25 mm) long on the top center of each bookmark. The child can move the bookmark so that the dark line is under the word that is being read.

The Story Racetrack

Write about what happened in the beginning, the middle, and the end of the story.

Name: _____

Title of story _____

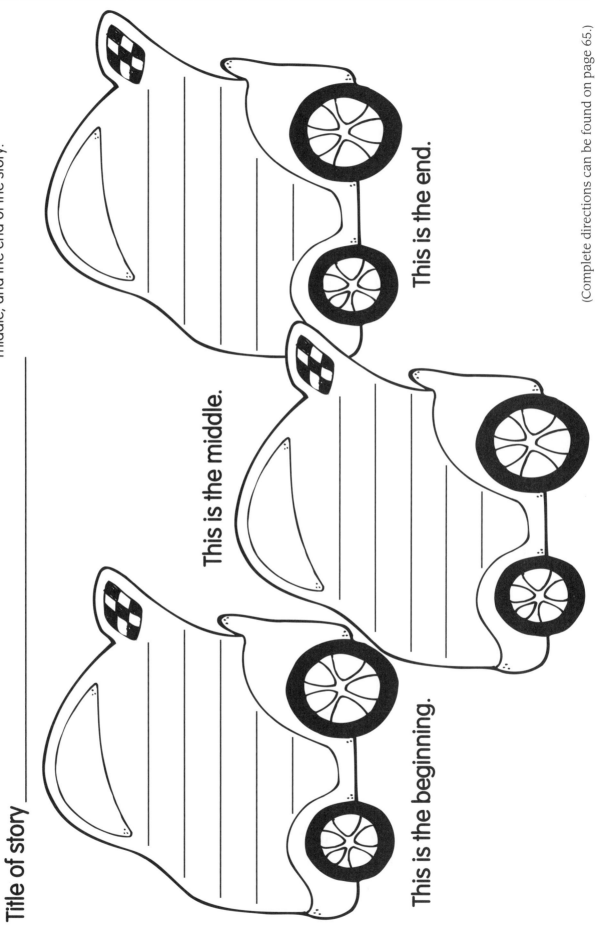

This is the end.

This is the middle.

This is the beginning.

(Complete directions can be found on page 65.)

Everyone Reads!

Story Pyramid

(Complete directions can be found on page 65.)

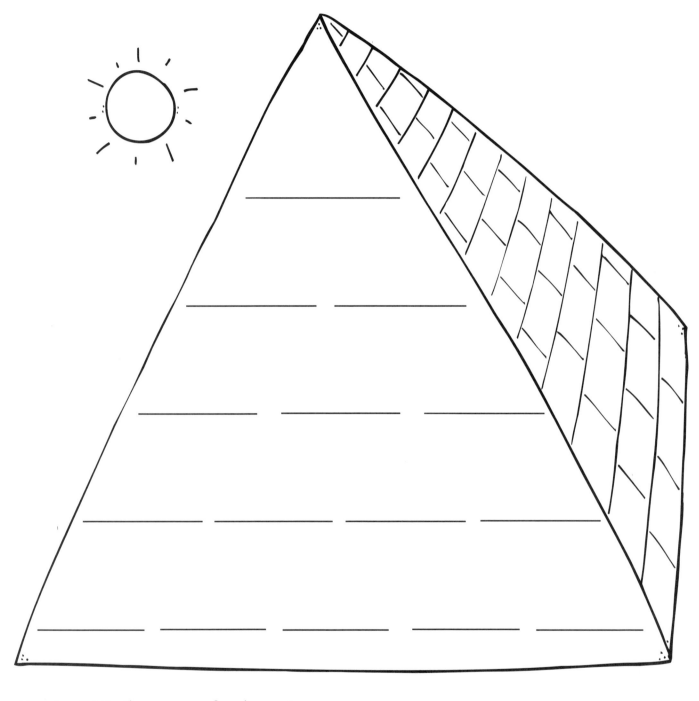

Line 1: Write the name of a character.

Line 2: Write 2 words that tell about the setting.

Line 3: Write 3 words that tell about the character.

Line 4: Write 4 words that tell about one event in the story.

Line 5: Write 5 words in a sentence that tells about the ending of the story.

Name _____

The Who, What, When, Where, and Why Reporter

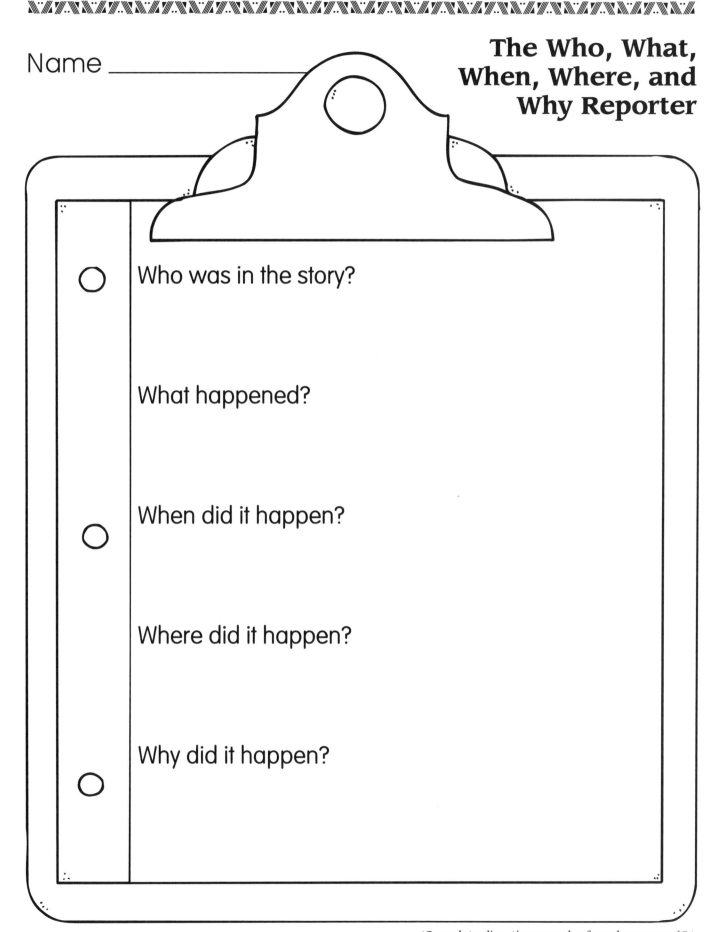

Who was in the story?

What happened?

When did it happen?

Where did it happen?

Why did it happen?

(Complete directions can be found on page 65.)

Name _____

(Complete directions can be found on page 65.)

Detailed Character Map
(Complete directions can be found on page 66.)

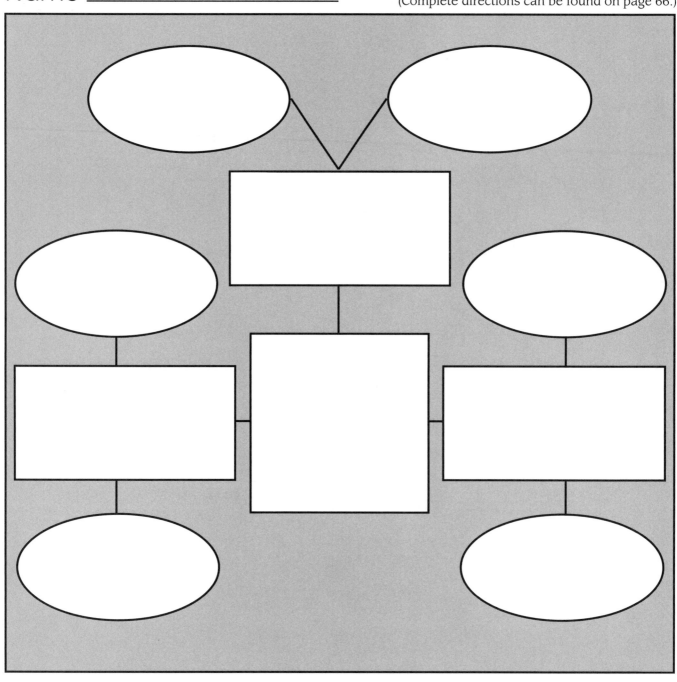

☐ Write the name of the character.

▭ Write words that describe the character.

⬭ How did the character show those qualities.

Directions: Cut out along the dotted lines.
Fold along the solid lines.

Comic Talk

(Complete directions can be found on page 66.)

75

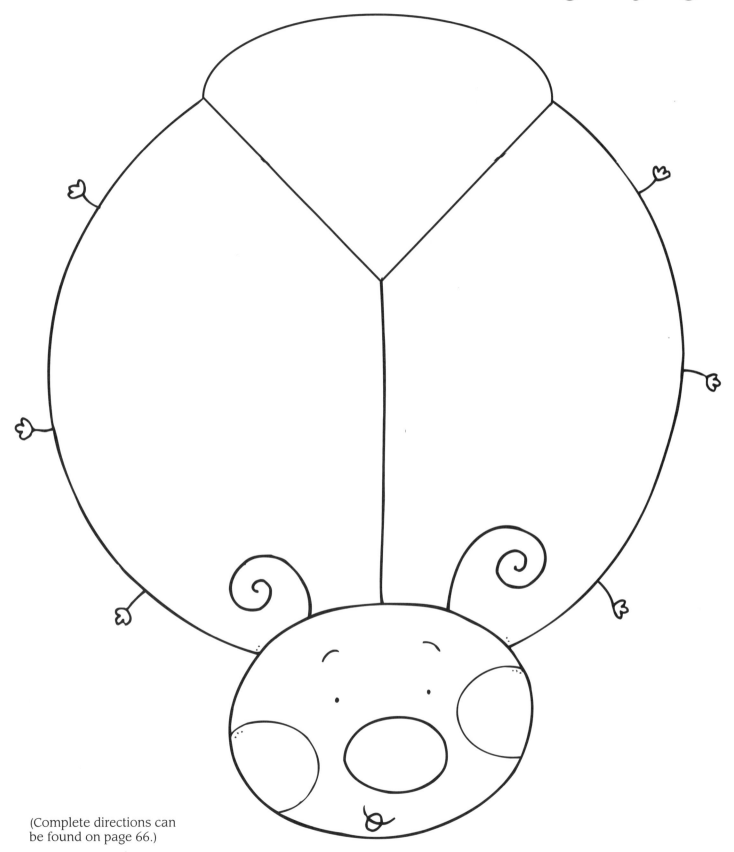

(Complete directions can
be found on page 66.)

Name _____

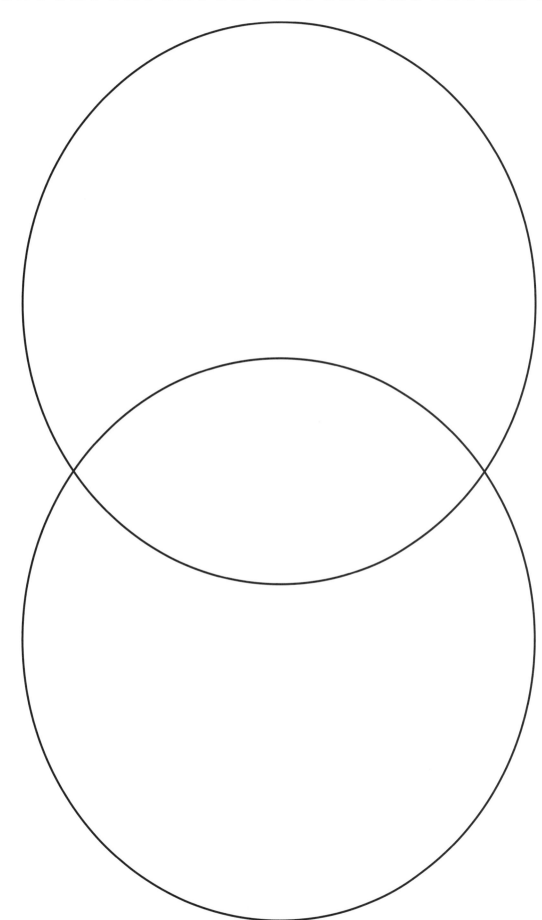

(Complete directions can be found on page 67.)

KWL Chart
(Complete directions can be found on page 67.)

K – What I know.	**W** – What I want to know.	**L** – What I learned.

- -

Storyboard

Directions: Draw pictures or write words to help remember sequential events in the story.

1.	2.	3.
4.	5.	6.

(Complete directions can be found on page 67.)

Name _____

Directions: Write the title and main idea on the cone. Write a supporting detail in each scoop of ice cream.

(Complete directions can be found on page 67.)

Tic-Tac-Toe Notes
(Complete directions can be found on page 68.)

Game Board Notes

GO →   →   →   →   →

The
End

(Complete directions can be found on page 67.)

My To Do List:

My Weekly Assignment Planner:

Monday

Tuesday

Wednesday

Thursday

Friday

(Complete directions can be found on page 68.)

(Complete directions can be found on page 68.)

Building Fluency

Develop Decoding Skills and
Increase High-Frequency Word Recognition

Fluency is the ability to read words fast, accurately, with comprehension, and with expression. To achieve this, children need to learn how to decode words with regular patterns (common word families or word chunks), and they need to be able to instantly identify high-frequency words that may follow irregular patterns.

Beginning readers and struggling readers recognize very few words instantly. Through repeated exposure to the same words, and with multi-sensory experiences, children can significantly increase the number of words they are able to instantly identify. The 25 most common words (see page 84) make up about one-fourth to one-third of all reading material. Instant recognition of these words can also have an incredible impact on increasing a child's reading speed and comprehension.

Tactile Words

Introduce new words and then allow children to mold the words with clay (see page 47, Clay—High-Frequency Words). Offer other opportunities for children to "feel" the new words (see page 27, Multi-Sensory Writing Center).

Teach new high-frequency words in isolation first. Provide fun activities that center around the individual word. After the children are familiar with the new word, then have them start to use the word in context.

Enlarged Versions of the Printed Page

Providing children with an enlarged version of the page can be extremely helpful. Children can use highlighters to mark difficult words. New words can also be highlighted in the text prior to reading the selection. This helps remind children of the new word.

My Own Word/Picture Dictionary

Provide each child with a notebook that has an alphabet letter in the upper right-hand corner of every page (one letter per page). As children learn new words, they can add them to the correct page. The children should write the word, illustrate it if possible, and be encouraged to use the word in a sentence.

As the words begin to fill up the dictionary, the child's self-confidence will increase. It is rewarding when children actually "see" that they are learning to read and understand more and more words! Children will also benefit from looking up words in their own dictionaries.

Bingo and Lotto Games

Teacher-made (or commercially purchased) bingo and lotto games are always fun for children to play and are excellent activities for reinforcing high-frequency word recognition. Bingo games help children recognize words "auditorily," while lotto games help children to match or "visually" recognize words.

Sight Word Hopscotch

Use a discarded plastic window shade or vinyl tablecloth with a permanent black marker. Draw a hopscotch grid and write a high-frequency word in each section. The children can jump on the words and say them as they "hop." The children can also use beanbags and toss each one onto a word. This activity provides a visual, auditory, and kinesthetic learning experience.

Word Wall Excitement

Many teachers are now using word walls—there is no doubt about their effectiveness for reinforcing words and for motivating young readers. Read all of the words every day! Each day the children will become more confident and their reading speed will increase.

Be creative with the classroom word walls. For example, tape the cards to streamers for a circus theme. Other options would be to place each word in an alphabet planet so that the Big "Bb" planet would have the words *big*, *but*, and *boy* on the planet, or make an "Around the Town" word wall, having each letter be a building with the words being displayed in the windows.

– en
ten
hen
men
then
when

Word Chunks

It is an exciting time for children when they realize that not every word needs to be learned as an entirely new word! Many words have "chunks," or phonograms that are already known. For example, the child has learned to read the word *at*, and now he realizes that the word *at* can easily be turned into the words *cat*, *hat*, and *rat*.

Make banners or posters with word chunks written on the top and add words as the children are able to identify them.

Word Substitution Games

This activity is extremely useful when introducing a new theme, topic, or a new high-frequency word.

Make up several sentences in which the same key word has been omitted. As each paragraph progresses, each sentence should reveal more clues about the meaning of the key word. Using an overhead projector, show the paragraph one sentence at a time to the children. Record several students' responses as they predict what goes in the blanks.

Example: The answer to these sentences is "dog."

A _____ can be a fun. Everybody would like a _____.

If you have a _____, you can do many things together with it.

You can go to the park with your _____. A _____ can play fetch with you.

A _____ is someone who likes you.

A _____ can chew bones.

Important High-Frequency Words for Children to Learn

The 25 Most Common Words	The 100 Most Used Words			
	List 1	List 2	List 3	List 4
1. the	and	are	all	away
2. and	boy	at	am	blue
3. a	can	but	ask	every
4. to	come	could	do	father
5. in	did	doing	down	from
6. you	girl	eat	for	green
7. of	go	get	good	had
8. it	help	going	has	house
9. is	like	he	have	how
10. he	man	here	him	in
11. she	mother	it	is	just
12. that	not	look	keep	little
13. was	out	make	let	much
14. for	play	new	me	need
15. I	read	now	must	old
16. his	see	one	my	put
17. her	the	said	of	ran
18. they	this	she	over	red
19. with	to	they	so	ride
20. are	us	two	some	run
21. be	want	use	that	there
22. but	will	we	them	walk
23. at	with	were	thing	was
24. one	work	would	what	went
25. said	you	your	why	yellow

Increasing Speed, Expression, and Comprehension

Learning to recognize high-frequency words and regular word patterns definitely helps to increase fluency. There are many fun activities that can enrich a child's reading experience, build fluency, increase reading expression, and strengthen comprehension skills. Incorporate some of the following ideas into your reading lesson plans.

Choral Stories/Readers Theatre

Choose a story that requires the children to read a part, or where they can join in and say the refrain in the appropriate places in the story. For example, while reading "The Three Pigs," the whole class would chorus, "Not by the hair on my chinny-chin-chin." After participating in the storytelling, the children will love to read the story on their own.

Overhead Reading

Have the whole class read a book aloud by using the overhead projector. The reading can be done together, individually, or silently. The whole class can enjoy a book together at the same time. Circle the words that are new, or the words that the children have difficulty decoding. Read and reread the story to increase fluency. When the children can read the text with ease, invite the children to act out the story while others read the pages aloud. Now the activity becomes "story theatre."

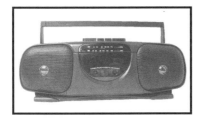

Taped Reading

Have the children record a story on the tape recorder. Play back the recording so that the children can check their oral reading as they reread the story silently. Listening to themselves read is a fascinating way to motivate children to practice and improve their reading skills.

Watch the Reader

Have the children in a reading group listen to the teacher read. Ask them to follow along silently and catch any mistakes. Read slowly. Keep the children engaged by asking their help with words or by misreading every fifth word. Children will giggle over catching the teacher making a mistake, and at the same time they will become more aware of accurate reading.

Unison Reading

Select a favorite story. Have one of the children read the story to the rest of the class or have two children stand in front of the class and take turns reading. It is also fun for the whole class to read in unison. The children will have the thrill of performing and at the same time will get practice in reading.

Switch Around Reading

Group the children for reading in a variety of different ways. At times, work could be done in pairs or small groups. The children can select their own partners or the teacher can pair together the good and poor readers to take turns reading a story, working on word drills, or playing a reading game.

The regular reading groups could meet with a child as the leader. The leader would have the honor of sitting in the teacher's chair and telling each child when to read. The leader would also make sure the reading is done correctly.

Working with peers introduces a new relevancy in reading and breaks the routine of the usual teacher-dominated reading situations.

Talking Books

Have each group of children make a large book cover from construction paper for a book. The book cover forms the body of a "book person." Ask the children to make and attach the paper head, arms, and legs to the body. Place the book people on the wall around the room. Cut out paper speech bubbles for each one. Invite the children to write out the words they think the book characters are saying. Each book character should tell something about the story, speaking in the first person. Each monologue is then added near the mouth of each character. The book people will encourage the children to read the actual books.

Poetry Day

Set aside a day to enjoy poetry. Recommend books of poetry for the children to read. Have the children read aloud a favorite poem. After sharing their favorite poems, have the children write their own couplets about a person, event, holiday, or object, or give the children the first line and ask them to rhyme the second line. Duplicate the writings and give each child a copy. A better appreciation for poetry will be the result.

I like you!

And you like me, too!

You are my best friend,

For always, the end!

I want to read a book . . .

about how to cook

Great Read-Aloud Books

Abuela. Arthur Dorros. (Dutton, 1991)
The Adventures of Taxi Dog. Debra Barracca. (Dial, 1990)
Alison's Zinnia. Anita Lobel. (Greenwillow, 1990)
Amelia's Road. Linda Jacobs. (Altman, Lee & Low Books, 1995)
Animals Should Definitely Not Wear Clothing. Judi Barrett. (Atheneum, 1970)
Anno's Counting House. Mitsumasa Anno. (Philomel Books, 1982)
Araminta's Paint Box. Karen Ackerman. (Atheneum, 1990)
Bearsie Bear and the Surprise Sleepover Party. Bernard Waber. (Houghton Mifflin, 1997)
Blueberries for Sal. Robert McCloskey. (Viking Books, 1976)
Brown Bear, Brown Bear, What Do You See? Bill Martin Jr. (Henry Holt and Co., 1996)
Bunny Cakes. Rosemary Wells. (Puffin Books, 2000)
Bunny Money. Rosemary Wells. (Puffin Books, 2000)
Buz. Richard Egielski. (HarperCollins Children's Books, 1995)
Cloudy with a Chance of Rain. Judi Barret. (Aladdin, 1982)
The Chanukkah Guest. Eric A. Kimmel. (Holiday House, 1990)
Charlotte's Web. E. B. White. (HarperTrophy, 1974)
Chicka Chicka Boom Boom. Bill Martin Jr. (Simon & Schuster, 1989)
Chicken Sunday. Patricia Polacco. (Philomel Books, 1992)
Dinorella: A Prehistoric Fairy Tale. Pamela Duncan Edwards. (Hyperion, 1997)
Elizabeth and Larry. Marilyn Sadler. (Simon & Schuster, 1990)
Elmer. David McKee. (HarperCollins, 1989)
Emily and the Enchanted Frog. Helen V. Griffith. (Greenwillow, 1989)
Eppie M. Says. Olivier Dunrea. (Simon & Schuster, 1990)
The Enormous Crocodile. Roald Dahl. (Knopf Books, 2000)
Everybody Needs a Rock. Byrd Baylor. (Atheneum, 1974)
Feathers for Lunch. Lois Ehlert. (Harcourt, 1990)
First Day Jitters. Julie Danneberg. (Charlesbridge Publishing, 2000)
Flossie and the Fox. Patricia McKissack. (Dutton Books, 1986)
The Foot Book. Dr. Seuss. (Random House, 1968)
Gathering the Sun: An Alphabet in Spanish and English. Alma Flor Ada. (Rayo, 1997)
Give Me a Sign! What Pictograms Tell Us Without Words. Tiphaine Samoyault.
    (Viking Books, 1997)
Good Driving, Amelia Bedelia. Peggy Parish. (HarperTrophy, 1996)
Goodnight Moon. Margaret Wise Brown. (HarperCollins, 1976)
The Great Kapok Tree. Lynne Cherry. (Gulliver Green, 1990)
Green Eggs and Ham. Dr. Seuss. (Random House, 1968)
The Grey Lady and the Strawberry Snatcher. Molly Bang. (Simon & Schuster, 1984)
Growing Vegetable Soup. Lois Ehlert. (Harcourt, 1987)
The Handmade Alphabet. Laura Rankin. (Dial, 1991)
Hattie and the Fox. Mem Fox. (Simon & Schuster, 1987)
Hello, Mrs. Piggle-Wiggle. Betty MacDonald. (HarperCollins, 1957)
Hop on Pop. Dr. Seuss. (Random House, 1976)
Horace. Holly Keller. (Greenwillow, 1991)
I Do Not Want to Get Up Today. Dorothy Cantor. (Little Brown and Company, 2001)
I Know an Old Lady Who Swallowed a Fly. Simms Taback. (Viking, 1997)
If You Give a Moose a Muffin. Laura Numeroff. (Laura Geringer, 1991)
The Important Book. Margaret Wise Brown. (HarperTrophy, 1990)
In a Cabin in a Wood. Darcie McNally. (Cobblehill, 1991)

In the Tall, Tall Grass. Denise Fleming. (Henry Holt & Co., 1995)
James and the Giant Peach. Roald Dahl. (Puffin, 2000)
Julius, the Baby of the World. Kevin Henkes. (Greenwillow, 1990)
Knuffle Bunny: A Cautionary Tale. Mo Williams. (Hyperion, 2004)
Last Tales of Uncle Remus. Julius Lester. (Dial Books, 1994)
Lester's Dog. Karen Hesse. (Knopf Books, 1993)
Little Engine That Could. Watty Piper. (Grosset & Dunlap, 1978)
Little Pea. Amy Krouse Rosenthal. (Chronicle Books, 2005)
Little Red Riding Hood: A Newfangled Prairie Tale. Lisa Campbell Ernst.
        (Simon & Schuster, 1995)
Lon Po Po. Ed Young. (Philomel Books, 1989)
Ma Dear's Aprons. Patricia C. McKissack. (Atheneum, 1997)
Madeline. Ludwig Bemelmans. (Viking, 1958)
Make Way for Ducklings. Robert McCloskey. (Viking, 1941)
Millions of Cats. Wanda Gág. (Rebound by Sagebrush, 1999)
Miss Rumphius. Barbara Cooney. (Viking, 1982)
The Mitten. Jan Brett. (Putnam Juvenile, 1989)
The Mixed-Up Chameleon. Eric Carle. (HarperTrophy, 1988)
Mr. Popper's Penguins. Richard Atwater. (Little Brown, 1988)
The Mud Flat Olympics. James Stevenson. (Greenwillow Books, 1994)
My Memory String. Eve Bunting. (Clarion Books, 2000)
My Painted House, My Friendly Chicken, and Me. Maya Angelou. (Crown Books, 2003)
My Very First Mother Goose. Iona Opie. (Candlewick, 1999)
Nana Upstairs, Nana Downstairs. Tomie De Paola. (Putnam, 1975)
The Napping House. Audrey and Don Wood. (Harcourt, 1984)
The New Adventures of Mother Goose. Bruce Lansky. (Meadowbrook, 1993)
No, David! David Shannon. (Scholastic, 1998)
Olivia. Ian Falconer. (Atheneum, 2000)
Once Upon a Springtime. Jean Marzollo. (Econo-Clad Books, 1999)
One Fish, Two Fish, Red Fish, Blue Fish. Dr. Seuss. (Random House, 1976)
The Polar Express. Chris Van Allsburg. (Houghton Mifflin, 1985)
The Red Balloon. Albert Lamorisse. (Doubleday, 1967)
The Relatives Came. Cynthia Rylant. (Aladdin, 1993)
The Snowy Day. Ezra Jack Keats. (Viking, 1962)
Squirrels. Brian Wildsmith. (Oxford University Press, 1992)
Stellaluna. Janell Cannon. (Harcourt, 1993)
The Story of Babar. Jean de Brunhof. (Random House, 1937)
The Story of Ferdinand. Munro Leaf. (Viking, 1936)
Swimmy. Leo Lionni. (Knopf Books, 1992)
The Tree Little Pigs. James marshall. (Puffin Books, 1996)
This Is the House That Jack Built. Pam Adams. (Child's Play-International, 1990)
Town Mouse, Country Mouse. Jan Brett. (Putnam, 1994)
Two of Everything. Lily Toy Hong. (Albert Whitman & Company, 1992)
What Do You Do with a Tail Like This? Melinda Long. (Harcourt, 2003)
Why Mosquitoes Buzz in People's Ears. Verna Aardema. (Dial, 1975)
The World That Jack Built. Ruth Brown. (Dutton Books, 1991)
The 20th Century Children's Book Treasury: Picture Books and Stories to Read Aloud.
        Janet Schulman. (Knopf, 1998)
26 Letters and 99 Cents. Tana Hoban. (Greenwillow, 1987)

After the Story—
Increasing Comprehension Skills

Grab Bag

Decorate a paper bag. Fill the bag with cards that represent four or five different events in a story that the children have just finished reading. The cards can either be written sentences that describe the event or illustrated pictures of the events.

The children will then take turns drawing a card out of the bag. Using a pocket chart, or the ledge of the blackboard, the children decide as a group how to properly sequence and arrange the cards. When the small group of children have finished sequencing the cards, the rest of the children in the class then decide whether the small group has properly sequenced the cards. Finally, have the children retell the story using the sentence or picture cards as their guide.

Story Comics

After reading a story, have the children make a 4-panel comic strip that retells the important events in the story. Show the action of the characters and use balloons over their heads to indicate the speech of the characters. These comic strips can be duplicated and distributed to the class for fun reading.

Get a Glimpse of a Good Book

Ask each of the children to bring a shoebox to school. Have the children illustrate an interesting scene from the book they have just read. Have each child trim the drawing to fit inside one end of the box. Actual objects and cut outs can be added to the scene to give it a 3-D effect. Have an adult cut a small hole—1 inch (25 mm) in diameter at the opposite end of the box. Underneath the hole have the child print the book title and author's name. Place the cover back on the box.

The children will enjoy peeking through the hole and viewing the scene at the back of each box. Display all the "peek boxes" on a counter with the caption "Get a glimpse of a good book to read."

Room Reader

Take a memorable character from a recent story and have the class make up new adventures for that character. Write down what the children say and then make copies of the new version for the class. This experience gives children an opportunity to re-read their original "story" and helps them to gain a better understanding of the story and the vocabulary used in the story.

Big Book

Tell the class that they will be making an oversized book of a favorite story. Use heavy cardboard for the cover and inside pages. Choose a story that can be retold in about eight scenes and write on each page a description for each illustration. Divide the class into eight groups—each group creating a page for the book. When finished, let the children decide how the pages should be sequenced together to form the book.

Arranging Cards

After reading a favorite book to the class, gather responses from the children to the question, "Tell me one thing that you remember from the story?" All responses are accepted. Write each response on a large index card, or sentence strip, and then give the card to the student. Repeat this process until 10 to 12 responses have been recorded.

Have the children with the cards come up to the front of the classroom. Those children remaining in their seats must decide as a group how they want to arrange the cards in a meaningful way. There must be a consensus among the children. Any arrangement that makes sense, and that the group can defend, is acceptable.

Postcard

Copy the postcard below onto card stock, one per child. Have the children write a postcard to send to someone: to persuade them to read the story; or to a movie producer to convince them to make a movie of the story; or to the author to share what they liked about the story. On the other side of the postcard, have the children draw an appropriate illustration.

Your
stamp
here

Take-a-Picture

After a story has been read to the children, invite them to pretend that they are "photographers." They should take a picture of the most important part of the story by drawing it. The children can add captions to explain what is happening in their "photographs." Use the reproducible photo template at the bottom of the page.

Map-It-Out

Have the children draw a map of the "setting" for the story, or the main character's neighborhood, city, or room. For example, draw a map of the Hundred Acre Wood from Winnie-the-Pooh.

True or False?

Prepare statements about a selection the children have read. Have some of the statements be true and have some of the statements be false. Give each child a card with the word "true" written on one side, and the word "false" written on the other side. The cards can be laminated for durability. The children will respond to each of the statements being read by holding up their card to vote.

       Everyone Reads!

Book Cover

On a piece of blank paper, have the children design a new book cover for the story that they have been reading or have heard during story time. It can reflect something that has happened in the story, their favorite part of the story, a favorite character, or an appropriate picture for the book title.

TV Show

Announce to the children that they are going to create a television show from one of their reading selections. To begin, gather statements (one statement per child) that advance the plot of the story. Include the title page. The teacher and students should then organize the statements in proper sequence. A number is placed on each statement and handed back to each child. Have the children illustrate their own statements.

All papers are then put in order and taped together to make one long strip. The ends are taped to cardboard tubes as shown in the illustration below. Have two children turn the tubes in unison so the other children can watch their "TV show." A narrator can be used to tell the story. To add to the enjoyment of this activity, encourage the class to make a television from a cardboard box.

Re-Write The Ending

This activity can be completed in two different ways. First, have the children create an illustration of how the story ends. Then the children can either write and illustrate a new ending from a certain point in the story, or the children can take the original ending and extend it beyond the author's ending and then illustrate that ending.

Have the children fold an 8.5" x 11" (22 cm x 28 cm) paper in half. On the top of the paper they can illustrate the original ending. On the bottom half of the page have them illustrate the new ending.

Picture Book Murals

Before starting to work on the murals, divide the class into three or more groups. In their groups, encourage the children to write down 5 to 10 statements that tell the story. Then have them sequence the events and glue them in order onto a large piece of butcher paper. When the children finish this, then have them draw illustrations.

Alternatively, the activity can be accomplished in the same manner, with the exception of having the teacher help the children to generate the statements. Each group would sequence and illustrate the same statements. Younger children can illustrate and tell the teacher what is happening in their pictures.

Casting Director

After the children have read the story, ask them to list all of the characters and discuss their attributes and personalities. This can be done individually or as a class.

As a casting director, have the children cast the members of their class into the roles of the characters from the story. If appropriate, the casting director could try to cast the children according to similarities they may share with the characters from the story.

Those children cast as characters in the story might then enjoy trying to dramatize a scene or event from the story.

KWL Chart

K–What I know.	W–What I want to know.	L–What I learned.

Post-Reading Strategies

1. Make a vocabulary or spelling list of the new words from the story.

2. Discuss the story: How did you feel about the selection? Was it easy to read? Was it too difficult, or was it just right?

3. After reading the story, fill in the KWL chart on page 78.

4. Direct the children to go back and reread the sections that they may have had difficulty with while reading the first time.

5. Discuss: Did the children like story? Did they find it interesting? What did they learn from the story?

Message to Parents:
12 Ways to Build Your Child's Self-Esteem

Children who feel valued, loved, and appreciated tend to develop positive self-esteems. Children with a strong sense of self and who "like themselves" are more likely to work harder in school and strive for their own personal best.

1. **Praise and encourage.** Self-esteem is boosted by encouragement that comes from a parent. Also praise without words—hugs and kisses tell children they are loved. More than anything, children need to know that they have people who love them unconditionally!

2. **Sense of being unique.** All children need to know that they have special talents and strengths. Find opportunities to point out all the things that your child does well.

3. **Set realistic goals and expectations.** Children who do not experience success grow up only understanding failure. Assist your child in defining goals, in small steps, that you know can be achieved. A foundation of successful experiences builds confidence and a willingness to tackle new challenges.

4. **When failure happens,** and it will on occasion—be sure to help your child understand that a failure is only a temporary set-back, and a learning experience, and that you do not feel let down by the child.

5. **Teach problem solving and decision making skills.** Allowing your child to make decisions builds confidence. Your child can see that he is trusted. At the same time, teach him to prioritize, to think about consequences, and to plan ahead. These are lifelong skills that lead to good decision making.

6. **Teach tolerance.** Help children learn to value others with different backgrounds. Encourage them to see individual strengths.

7. **I'm a Valuable and Connected Person.** Teach your children how important they are to your family, to a sports team, and to a class. Children who feel connected, and have opportunities to be members of social groups, learn how to be strong functional adults.

8. **Teach social skills and manners.** Children who have been taught manners and have watched their parents model good social and conversational skills, will be able to have positive social interactions and relationships with others.

9. **Be respectful.** Children who are treated with respect will learn to respect others. Children should be spoken to and treated like intelligent and important people. They will grow up to be confident and trusting adults.

10. **Define limits and rules.** Children who have a clear understanding of what is expected will feel more secure. "Knowing" creates security, while "not knowing or understanding" creates feelings of insecurity.

11. **Provide many new experiences.** Children who are provided many and varied experiences are learning all sorts of ways to face new challenges. This gives the child a larger repertoire of skills to draw upon.

12. **Encourage respectful self-expression.** Children who are listened to and who receive respectful and thoughtful responses are taught that what they have to say is important and valued. It will also teach children to listen and speak respectfully to others.

Message to Parents:
15 Great Reading Tips for Parents

Parents can make an incredible difference in helping their child become a more successful reader. There are so many fun activities and ideas you can utilize to encourage and motivate your child to become a better reader.

1. **Read together everyday!** This can become a very special time shared with your child.

2. **Set a good example.** Let your child see you reading. Have lots of good reading material around the house.

3. **Visit the library often.** Children enjoy choosing new books to read. Take advantage of reading programs and other materials found at the library, such as books on tape or audio filmstrips.

4. **Read the same books.** Read your child's favorite books over and over again. This helps children learn to identify words in print and can help increase fluency.

5. **Let children make their own book selections.** Some popular books may not be a parent's first choice, but by allowing children to read what interests them can make reading more pleasurable.

6. **Stop while reading.** Stop and ask questions about the story or the illustrations. Discuss what is happening in the story or what the child thinks might happen next.

7. **Discuss vocabulary.** Talk about new words: what they mean, how they were used in the sentence, or make comparisons. For example, if the new word was "palace," discuss how a castle, a mansion, or a very big house might be like a palace.

8. **Work with large type.** Point to words as you read. This helps children identify words while reinforcing how to read from left to right.

9. **Read a variety of genres.** Read picture books, fairy tales, adventures, informational books, tall tales, and mysteries. This will help to expand the interests of your child.

10. **Books on tape or CD.** These can be listened to in the car, or the whole family can enjoy them together. Sometimes after a child has heard the story, they will want to read the book independently.

11. **Subscribe to a children's magazine.** There are many wonderful children's magazines. Subscribe to one of these in your child's name, because children love to receive mail. They will look forward to the arrival of the magazine and will be eager to start reading.

12. **Point out the importance of reading in the real world.** Talk about how people read menus, maps, food labels, directions, newspapers, video labels, brochures, cookbooks, street signs, billboards, addresses, and phone books.

13. **Extend the reading experience.** If your child is reading a book about animals, visit the zoo. If your child is reading a book about dinosaurs, visit a museum. If your children is reading a book about nature, take a walk together.

14. **Make your own books on tape.** Record a story together. Read with expression; use funny voices; read dramatically.

15. **Create a reading project.** When your child has finished reading a story, create a fun project that relates to the story. For example, cook something from the story, draw an illustration, or mold a clay sculpture.

Message to Parents:
15 Homework Tips that Really Work!

Completing homework can either be a good experience or it can be quite frustrating! By establishing some simple routines, helping your child to learn some organizational skills, and by being available, makes daily homework a more successful experience for everyone!

1. **Use an assignment planner.** This simple system will help your child remember to bring assignments home. Include a reward system for using the assignment planner.

2. **Establish a scheduled time for homework.** Establish a regular time when homework is to be done. Children will quickly get into the "habit" of doing homework on time.

3. **Establish an organized place where homework is completed.** Make sure this space is free of distractions—no TV, phone, or people coming and going.

4. **Readily available supplies.** Make sure that children have everything they may need when they begin their homework: sharpened pencils, crayons, ruler—or whatever special tools might be required for the assignments.

5. **Get organized.** Teach your children to use an organizer. Develop a system for storing school papers and keeping them organized. Fewer materials will get misplaced or lost!

6. **Have a snack.** Children who are hungry cannot concentrate as well. Make sure that your child has had a nutritious snack before beginning the homework.

7. **Keep old quizzes and tests.** Old quizzes and tests can become valuable tools for your child when studying for a new test or for reviewing end-of-chapter material.

8. **Be positive.** Completing homework can give children a sense of accomplishment and help them to feel successful. Establish a positive reward system.

9. **Review the assignments with your child and help prioritize tasks.** Teach your child to review what has to be accomplished before beginning. This helps children set priorities. It is often best for children to complete the work that is considered "hard" first. Save the "easy" homework for last.

10. **Be available.** It is not your job to do your child's homework. However, you should be available to answer questions and provide guidance when needed.

11. **Watch for failure or frustration.** Talk with your child's teacher immediately if you see that your child does not understand the assignments, or is becoming frustrated, or is not able to do the work without a large amount of assistance.

12. **Check child's assignments when finished.** This will allow you to see if your child is understanding the work that is being required. It will also make your child feel very proud when you look at the work and praise the accomplishments!

13. **Keep in touch with the teacher.** Make sure that regular communication is happening between home and school.

14. **Great trouble reading.** If your child has a difficult time reading the material required, ask the teacher about recording the text on tape for the children to listen to at home. You can also read the material with your child to improve their reading skills.

15. **Homework should not go on all night.** If homework is taking too long, talk to the teacher. Hours and hours of homework is not beneficial for a young child!